Fearless Em

Spark

Sensitivity Brilliance

Tackle Empathy Concerns, Cultivate the Power of Authenticity, Trigger Compassionate Actions, and Unleash Your True Potential

Devi Sunny

GRAB YOUR FREE GIFT BOOK

MBTI enumerates 16 types of people in the world. Each of us is endowed with different talents, which prove to be the innate strength of our personality. To understand the deeper psychology of your personality type, unique cognitive functions, and integrated personality growth path, you can scan the QR code below or visit www.clearcareer.in for a free download –

"Your Personality Strength Report"

Successful Intelligence Series

1) Book 1 **Grow Practical Mindset**
2) Book 2 **Grow Analytical Mindset**
3) Book 3 **Grow Creative Mindset**

Fearless Empathy Series

1) Book 1 **Set Smart Boundaries**
2) Book 2 **Master Mindful No**
3) Book 3 **Conquer Key Conflicts**
4) Book 4 **Build Emotional Resilience**
5) Book 5 **Develop Vital Connections**
6) Book 6 **Achieve Balanced Personality**

Clear Career Inclusive Series

1) Book 1 **Raising Your Rare Personality**
2) Book 2 **Upgrade as Futuristic Empaths**
3) Book 3 **Onboard as Inclusive Leaders**

Contents

About the Book

Being soft and sensitive in a competitive world is a challenge. Many people find it difficult not to keep pace with how power and influence are celebrated worldwide. Being practical and influential is an inherent strength for some people. It comes from a practical and analytical intelligence that one has to survive. But can softness and sensitivity be seen as a weakness? It is a weakness until it is understood as the basis of creative intelligence.

Recognizing that we are all energy beings, the key to success lies in efficiently accessing and managing our energy. Just as focusing sunlight through a concave lens creates fire, focused energy drives our actions. Intuitive feelers or empaths prefer to channel their energy into generating ideas, while sensors channel theirs into actions and analysts into effectiveness. Empaths or sensitive individuals possess an enhanced ability to experience emotions deeply. Depending on their circumstances, they express it through various outlets, such as arts or investment in people. Their sincerity is profound, yet when their empathetic efforts are not reciprocated, it can lead to resentment.

Sensitivity works in individuals, much like the multifaceted nature of fire, which provides warmth and light depending on its intensity and distance (focused energy). But when such people focus on dispensing warmth, there arises a natural risk of attracting narcissists who will use this energy, leaving sensitive folks vulnerable to depression and resentment. Therapists advocate radical acceptance, self-growth, and rewriting one's story for those recovering from narcissistic relationships. This advice underscores the importance of knowing where to focus energy. Encountering narcissists serves as a wake-up call to step out of complacency, break comfort zones, and share gifts with the world. Though recognized quite late at times, when empathy is not valued, sensitive individuals are prompted to redirect their energy toward more appreciative recipients.

Highly sensitive people often exhibit heightened creativity but require a conducive environment to thrive. They have natural creative intelligence, emphasizing the need for empaths to express their unique gifts. Unless they select a conducive environment and control their intensity and distance to balance their sensitivity, they cannot be at their best. A balance of practicality and effectiveness is essential for them to be respected and valued. Brilliance involves discerning where and how to apply sensitivity effectively. This book aims to explore the concept further.

Compassion, seen as potential energy, fuels action. Empaths, envisioning possibilities and imagining a better world, must step out of their comfort zones to bring their best to the world and to be valued. Sensitivity is a dynamic force that, when channeled effectively, can lead to a positive change. Understanding the nuances of energy focus, adapting to diverse situations, and embracing practicality and rationality are critical elements in fostering a harmonious and impactful existence.

Introduction

"If there is any one secret of success, it lies in the ability to get the other person's point of view and see things from his angle as well as your own."- Henry Ford.

Is success defined by income, influence, and internal happiness? While tangible and intangible factors contribute to measuring success, the critical elements often include practical, analytical, and creative intelligence. The absence of any of these components may lead to unfulfillment. Many individuals, regardless of wealth and influence, often turn to spirituality. Why? Spirituality emphasizes seeking God, encouraging compassion, and recognizing the oneness in all – essentially teaching sensitivity. Rich and famous figures engage in charity and form foundations for social contributions, finding happiness in such acts. This all boils down to empathy, a value associated with internal happiness, which is crucial in today's times. However, is the power of empathy underestimated nowadays? Despite an empathy deficit, why is its application lacking? Are we genuinely doing everything to maximize our potential for internal happiness? Examining our collective success as a race raises questions. Why do some individuals struggle to achieve success? Could it be due to a lack of understanding

– an inability to value everyone's strengths and learn from one another? Is success hindered by the failure to integrate practicality, creativity, and analytical thinking? Consider the role of empathy in this equation- is the lack of success of a thinking personality type linked to their reluctance to be practical and creative? Does a practical person's non-existent success stem from an unwillingness to be creative and analytical? And is a creative person's struggle the result of blocks in being practical and analytical? Our diverse world contains thinkers, doers, and creative individuals. Hesitation to include and appreciate these varied personalities leads to biases and resistance to inclusion and hampers integrated personality development. Recognizing and embracing this diversity may be the key to unlocking human potential and achieving a more prosperous and harmonious existence. In other words, empathy acts as a binding force.

"A human being is part of a whole, called by us the 'Universe' —a part limited in time and space. He experiences himself, his thoughts, and his feelings as something separated from the rest—a kind of optical delusion of his consciousness. This delusion is a kind of prison for us, restricting us to our personal desires and affection for a few persons nearest us. Our task must be to free ourselves from this prison by widening our circles of compassion to embrace all living creatures and the whole of nature in its beauty." - **Albert Einstein.**

These profound words come from one of the world's most intelligent minds. If we fail to succeed, could it reflect our failure to embrace inclusivity? Empathy is immensely relevant and a powerful force for positive change. A lack of empathy in the world suggests that those lacking empathy haven't been taught how to exercise it or that those possessing empathy aren't acting on it sufficiently.

So, who are these individuals who possess empathy naturally as a strength? They are personality types with high scores in interpersonal and intrapersonal intelligence. Usually called empaths, they possess an innate skill of understanding. Some of them have high sensitivity and are therefore called Highly Sensitive People. They also have high creative intelligence, which makes them suitable in areas where creativity is essential. The healing impact of the arts is undeniable, and artists can serve as educators in empathy. However, in a world where the value of the arts is underrated, achieving internal happiness and complete success becomes challenging. Engaging in art, rather than merely observing or experiencing it, is where true happiness emerges – a concept evident by the contentment experienced by creative individuals, often identified by Daniel Kahneman as System 1 fast thinkers. Creativity flourishes best when one is at ease. Yet, for creative individuals to succeed, they must navigate sustaining analytical and practical criteria. Earning and influence become critical for them to thrive in a world that may not fully appreciate the value of their contributions. Creative minds encounter both internal and external challenges. While they act as healers for the world, the intensifying global competition often pushes them into System 2 thinking, inducing anxiety. The unfamiliarity surrounding the nature of creation results in ideas usually being dismissed as impractical until proven through practical implementation. Those envisioning a better world face skepticism until they substantiate their ideas as working and value-generating models. In navigating these challenges, creative individuals contribute to the world's progress while seeking validation and understanding from a society that may not always grasp the transformative power of their ideas.

"Great spirits have always found violent opposition from mediocre minds. The latter cannot understand it when a man does not thoughtlessly submit to hereditary prejudices but honestly and courageously uses his intelligence." - **Albert Einstein.**

Certain creative individuals often lean towards non-conformity. Following established norms may stifle their creative mindset. However, their divergence from the mainstream can expose them to many challenges. To overcome these hurdles, they must tap into their hidden courage, be educated on leveraging their strength and warmth appropriately, and embrace the wisdom of being free-spirited, as advocated by Swami Vivekananda: "Dare to be free, dare to go as far as your thought leads, and dare to carry that out in your life." According to Daniel Goleman, author of Emotional Intelligence, empathy involves a willingness to support others by taking action and understanding their needs or experiences.

"Self-absorption in all its forms kills empathy, let alone compassion. When we focus on ourselves, our world contracts as our problems and preoccupations loom large. But when we focus on others, our world expands. Our own problems drift to the periphery of the mind, and so seem smaller, and we increase our capacity for connection - or compassionate action." - **Daniel Goleman,** Social Intelligence: The New Science of Human Relationships.

Some of the intuitive Feelers are introverts. Their primary cognitive function or growth function is authenticity. Since they prefer to keep to themselves, they don't choose to connect as compared to extroverted individuals. But if they could grow beyond their natural preferences, it can cause wonders for themselves, and their natural gifts will benefit many. They should learn to use their power of authenticity in healing or creative roles. Otherwise, their energy would be misspent.

Contrary to the conventional view, Prof. Paul Bloom recommends rational, compassionate actions in "Against Empathy," noting that an empathic approach can lead to biases by spotlighting specific cases. Empathy tends to decrease from individual to mass suffering.

Other challenges include empathy traps and fatigue, where givers may feel drained or used and run the risk of becoming targets of narcissism.

"Givers have to set limits because takers rarely do." - **Henry Ford.**

The challenges of applying empathy raise a crucial question: Is there an intelligent, effective way to employ sensitivity and understand its impact on oneself and others? This book explores the possibilities of empathy, unraveling the intricacies of intelligent sensitivity and its role in achieving success for both the giver and the receiver.

1. Faces of Empathy

"If your emotional abilities aren't in hand if you don't have self-awareness, if you are not able to manage your distressing emotions, if you can't have empathy and have effective relationships, then no matter how smart you are, you are not going to get very far."-Daniel Goleman.

Anand Malligavad, an engineer in Bengaluru, India, transformed from an unlikely candidate to a leading figure in lake conservation in response to the city's water crisis. After an accidental encounter with a polluted lake in 2017, Malligavad proposed to his company, Sansera Engineering, that he would restore a 36-acre lake if funded. Despite initial skepticism, he delved into ancient Chola dynasty techniques, dating back 1,500 years, to manage lakes. He secured a $100,000 grant and restored Kyalasanahalli Lake in 45 days.

Over the next seven years, Malligavad rejuvenated 35 lakes in Bengaluru, covering 800 acres and holding 106 million gallons of water. His efforts transformed the landscape and raised the groundwater level by about eight feet. Bengaluru, once known for its natural lakes, now faces a severe water shortage due to urbanization and lake encroachments. Malligavad's methods involve creating separate lagoons and mud walls to direct excess water and utilizing Chola practices like trapping sludge with carved stones.

Despite facing opposition from landowners and illegal encroachers, Malligavad's determination led him to become a national conservation expert. His success has earned him advisory roles in multiple states, with governments entrusting him to revive hundreds of lakes. Bengaluru's water shortage of 172 million gallons per day, set to double by 2030, emphasizes the urgency of Malligavad's work. His vision extends beyond water bodies as he works on transforming landfills into forests, aiming to reclaim a hundred thousand lakes during his lifetime, underlining the irreplaceable importance of water.

What inspired Anand to go the extra mile? Not only did he initiate the work, but he also went the extra mile by learning the necessary techniques, persuading his company to allocate Corporate Social Responsibility funds, and personally executing the project, viewing it as his life mission. What if he had abandoned his initial efforts to convince the company to release funds? With the necessary financial support, the restoration project was possible, even if Anand had the willingness to undertake it. It is evident that though individuals possess varying levels of empathy, only some persevere until they bring about meaningful change.

Anand, the 'Lake Man of India,' attributes his inspiration to childhood memories of his village and the time he spent near the lake adjacent to his school. The villagers heavily relied on the lake for sustenance and irrigation, underscoring its vital role in their lives.

When translated into action, empathy transcends mere understanding, evolving into a potent force that holds immense value through the causes it champions. Think of it like a safety pin: dormant and insignificant when idle but invaluable when called upon to secure and mend. Empathy resembles this safety pin, serving as a conduit that connects meaningful actions, fostering positive change and impact. Just as a safety pin has the potential to hold things together, empathy finds its true power in bridging divides and fostering connections that uplift and unite.

"Sensitivity is a sign of strength. It's not about toughening up; it's about smartening up."- **Marie Forleo**.

Is empathy the same as sensitivity? What is the difference? Let's find out.

Types of Empathy

Empathy, a multifaceted capacity deeply ingrained in social, cognitive, and emotional processes, is fundamental to human interaction. Rooted in the Greek word "empatheia," empathy involves understanding others' emotions and thoughts, extending beyond the compulsion to help. It includes recognizing others' emotional states, often linked to our ability to mimic.

16

Empathy encompasses various forms, such as cognitive, emotional, somatic, and spiritual empathy. While compassion, sympathy, pity, and emotional contagion are similar to empathy, they are distinct concepts. Conversely, alexithymia involves struggling to grasp one's own emotions. Empathy comprises affective empathy, which emotionally responds to others, and cognitive empathy, which understands others' viewpoints.

All types of empathy serve unique functions, fostering connections and encouraging prosocial behavior. Cognitive empathy aids in comprehending diverse viewpoints, while emotional empathy involves experiencing others' emotions. Compassionate empathy merges both, actively assisting others in need. Self-empathy, often overlooked, entails recognizing and validating our feelings and needs, promoting personal well-being and resilience. Somatic empathy involves feeling someone else's physical pain, like experiencing pain when witnessing someone hurt. Spiritual empathy entails a direct connection with a higher being or consciousness, akin to enlightenment achieved through meditation.

"The great gift of human beings is that we have the power of empathy; we can all sense a mysterious connection to each other." - **Meryl Streep.**

Empaths and Sensitivity

Empaths and highly sensitive people (HSPs) share many characteristics, but the two have distinct differences.

Understanding these differences can help individuals better understand themselves and navigate their sensitivities.

Both empaths and HSPs have a low threshold for stimulation, requiring ample alone time and sensitivity to light, sound, and smell. They often prefer quiet environments and have a rich inner life. While highly sensitive people are typically introverts, empaths can be introverts or extroverts, though most lean towards introversion.

What sets empaths apart is their ability to sense subtle energy, absorbing it from others and their surroundings into their bodies. This deep sensitivity allows them to experience the energies around them intensely, often internalizing the feelings and pain of others. They may struggle to differentiate between their emotions and those of others, leading to emotional overwhelm. Additionally, some empaths have profound spiritual and intuitive experiences, such as communicating with animals, nature, and inner guides.

It's important to note that being an empath and a highly sensitive person is not mutually exclusive; many individuals embody both traits simultaneously. On an empathic spectrum, empaths are at the highest end, while highly sensitive people fall slightly lower. Empaths - those with strong empathy but who are not HSPs- occupy the middle of the spectrum, while individuals with empathy-deficient disorders like narcissists, sociopaths, and psychopaths are at the lowest end.

Sensitivity and empathy are invaluable gifts, particularly in today's world. Empaths and HSPs have the potential to make significant contributions, but they need to learn to harness their abilities and protect their energy.

"The most beautiful people we have known are those who have known defeat, known suffering, known struggle, known loss, and have found their way out of the depths. These persons have an appreciation, a sensitivity, and an understanding of life that fills them with compassion, gentleness, and a deep loving concern. Beautiful people do not just happen." - **Dr. Elisabeth Kübler-Ross.**

Traits of Empaths

Empaths are highly sensitive, naturally inclined towards giving, spiritually open, and attentive listeners. They absorb the emotions of others, feeling them intensely, which can lead to emotional exhaustion. Many empaths are introverted, overwhelmed by crowds, and preferring one-on-one or small-group interactions. Their intuition is profound, guiding them through life's complexities and aiding in forming positive relationships while avoiding energy vampires. Empaths require alone time to recharge, as being around others can be draining.

Intimate relationships can overwhelm empaths, as they fear losing their identity. Their sensitivity makes them targets for energy vampires, draining their emotional and physical energy. However, nature replenishes them, offering solace and rejuvenation. Empaths possess highly tuned senses, which can become overwhelmed by excessive stimuli. Despite their big hearts and desire to alleviate others' pain, empaths may give too much, neglecting their well-being.

Empaths must prioritize self-care, including time management, setting boundaries, meditation, and spending time in nature. Recognizing and honoring their unique needs is essential for maintaining emotional balance and communicating effectively with loved ones. Being an empath is a gift, but it requires proactive self-care to thrive in a world that can significantly benefit from their empathic presence.

Cognitive Functions of Empaths

Empaths are Intuitive & Feeling types. According to MBTI, they are INFP, INFJ, ENFP, and ENFJ Personality Types. Their Cognitive Functions are as follows:

Introverted Feeling (Fi) is INFP strength, and ENFP growth is based on the development of Fi.

INFPs are Introverted Intuitive Feeling and Perceiving types.

Introverted Feeling is the function that brings authenticity to a person since this function deals with morals and what the person truly believes. This function makes people value their existence, life, and values. Value-based thinking with their sets of beliefs can be the driver of their actions. A developed Fi will evaluate all questions about their beliefs and upgrade their understanding level.

Extraverted Intuition (Ne) is ENFP strength; INFP growth is based on the development of Ne.

ENFPs are extroverted and intuitive, as well as feeling and perceiving types.

Extroverts' intuition helps them ideate and discern multiple possibilities by connecting the events and actions of others. This function type's optimistic, curious, and creative side provides leverage to outsmart others in roles fueled by creativity. They demonstrate a remarkable ability to swiftly grasp and adjust to unfamiliar circumstances.

Introverted Intuition (Ni) is INFJ strength; ENFJ growth is based on the development of Ni.

INFJs are Introverted, Intuitive, Feeling, and Judging types.

The Introverted Intuition function makes a personality type extremely aware of the interconnectedness of actions in the world and their future implications. This function makes people highly aware of situations waiting to happen before their actual occurrence, envisaging patterns, possibilities, and impacts on the future. Their thoughts are so interweaved that with one actual event, they unconsciously get insights that lead to "Aha" moments. They can draw patterns from the information received and usually caution those around them of forthcoming situations and convince them to change their course of action.

Extroverted Feeling (Fe) is ENFJ strength, and INFJ growth is based on the development of Fe.
ENFJs are Extroverted, Intuitive, Feeling & Judging Types Extroverted Feeling aids people in ensuring harmony in social groups they belong to, where they are usually found actively spreading joy. Personality types with this function, whether in a dominant or assisting mode, will consciously work towards making people happy, sometimes to their detriment, all because they need to feel good about themselves.

Intelligence of Empaths
In 1983, Howard Gardner, a prominent psychologist from Harvard University, introduced the groundbreaking theory of multiple intelligences in his seminal work, "Frames of Mind: The Theory of Multiple Intelligences." Gardner introduced the notion that intelligence is not a unitary concept but rather a multifaceted spectrum, comprising a myriad of cognitive capabilities and talents.

His theory outlined nine unique forms of intelligence, highlighting the diverse array of cognitive skills and competencies inherent in human functioning. From linguistic and logical-mathematical intelligence to musical and interpersonal intelligence, Gardner's framework provided a comprehensive understanding of the multifaceted nature of human intellect.

Since its inception, the concept of multiple intelligences has undergone extensive development and expansion, permeating various fields, especially in learning design and education. Educators utilize Gardner's theory to create inclusive teaching methods tailored to individual strengths and learning styles, fostering a more holistic approach to education. Moreover, integrating multiple intelligences with personality testing offers individuals valuable insights into their aptitudes and propensities, guiding them in career choices and personal development endeavors.

INFPs, ENFPs, INFJs, and ENFJs exhibit distinct patterns of intelligence aligned with their personality types:

1. INFP (Introverted, Intuitive, Feeling, Perceiving): **Intrapersonal Intelligence:** INFPs exhibit exceptional intrapersonal intelligence, characterized by their deep insight into their own emotions, motivations, and values. They excel in self-reflection, introspection, and trusting their intuition to guide them.

2. ENFP (Extraverted, Intuitive, Feeling, Perceiving): **Interpersonal Intelligence:** ENFPs exhibit remarkable interpersonal intelligence, excelling in communication, empathy, and understanding the emotions and motivations of others. They thrive in building meaningful connections and inspiring others.

3. INFJ (Introverted, Intuitive, Feeling, Judging):

Interpersonal Intelligence: INFJs are adept at interpersonal intelligence and deeply understand others' emotions and motivations. They excel in communication, conflict resolution, and fostering harmonious relationships.

4. ENFJ (Extraverted, Intuitive, Feeling, Judging):

Interpersonal Intelligence: ENFJs showcase invaluable interpersonal intelligence, marked by their outstanding communication prowess, empathy, and capacity to inspire and motivate others. They thrive in leadership positions, adept at cultivating collaboration and fostering harmony within groups.

These personality types leverage their unique cognitive functions to navigate the world, contributing their respective intelligence to interpersonal dynamics and personal growth.

Empathically intelligent people are shaped by a process that includes three forms of empathy: cognitive, relational (emotional), and sacrificial (compassionate actions). These individuals become more dedicated to the well-being and growth of themselves and others, understanding that these goals are not separate. This mindset aligns with successful businesses as it prioritizes solving customer problems effectively. In the realm of design thinking, empathy plays a pivotal role, as a deficiency in empathy can lead to product failures.

"The main tenet of design thinking is empathy for the people you're trying to design for. Leadership is exactly the same thing — building empathy for the people that you're entrusted to help."- **David M. Kelley, IDEO.**

IDEO's Human-Centered Design Toolkit underscores the critical role of empathy in design thinking, defining it as a "profound comprehension of the challenges and circumstances encountered by the individuals for whom you are designing." Empathy necessitates delving into people's obstacles, revealing their unspoken needs and aspirations that shape their actions. Achieving empathy mandates a comprehensive grasp of one's surroundings, roles, and engagements within them to connect with one's experiences authentically.

Mapping Brilliance

Identify your MBTI personality type and map your strengths using the Multiple Intelligence Theory.

2. Challenges of Sensitive People

"Although HSPs may have been told they are "too sensitive," the truth is that the proliferation of insensitive values has created a world on the brink of disaster. Our only hope for saving the planet is sensitive people-- being role models and leading the way, to increase compassion and kindness toward all sentient beings on the planet."- Ted Zeff.

Maya Angelou, revered as both an author and a civil rights activist, experienced a profound journey from silence to an influential voice that resonated globally. Her decision to stop speaking stemmed from a traumatic event in her childhood—a brutal rape at the age of seven by her mother's boyfriend. The trauma was compounded by the swift but seemingly justified retribution exacted upon her attacker by her family, leading young Maya to believe her voice had lethal power.

In the aftermath, Maya fell into a silence that lasted for five years, a manifestation of selective mutism induced by the trauma. However, this silence became a transformative period of intense observation and learning. Immersed in literature during her muted years, Maya honed her understanding of human experiences, laying the foundation for her later literary prowess.

Highly Sensitive People (HSPs)

Sensory Processing Sensitivity (SPS) is a personality trait characterized by heightened sensitivity to physical, social, and emotional stimuli. Coined by psychologists Elaine and Arthur Aron, individuals with a high SPS are termed Highly Sensitive Persons (HSPs), constituting approximately 15-20% of the population. HSPs demonstrate increased emotional reactivity and engage in deeper cognitive processing, often pausing to assess novel situations. The Arons developed the Highly Sensitive Person Scale (HSPS) questionnaire to measure SPS.

While some researchers associate high SPS with adverse outcomes, such as heightened anxiety or stress, others suggest its potential benefits, including greater responsiveness to both positive and negative influences. It's important to note that SPS is not considered a disorder but a natural variation in human temperament.

The trait of SPS encompasses a spectrum of sensitivity levels, with individuals exhibiting varying degrees of responsiveness to stimuli. Understanding and acknowledging SPS can help individuals navigate their environments more effectively, recognize their unique sensitivities, and utilize coping strategies tailored to their needs. Ultimately, acknowledging and accepting SPS as a valid aspect of human diversity fosters greater understanding and support for individuals with heightened sensitivity.

"We are a package deal, however. Our trait of sensitivity means we will also be cautious, inward, needing extra time alone. Because people without the trait (the majority) do not understand that, they see us as timid, shy, weak, or that greatest sin of all, unsociable. Fearing these labels, we try to be like others. But that leads to our becoming over-aroused and distressed. Then that gets us labeled neurotic or crazy, first by others and then by ourselves."- **Elaine N. Aron.**

An article in *Positivepsychology.com* explores the concept of mirror neurons and their impact on human learning, cognition, and empathy. Mirror neurons fire when an individual acts and observes someone else performing the same action. They are believed to be fundamental to human learning and social interaction, enabling us to imitate and understand the behavior of others. Mirror neurons are pivotal in our capacity to empathize with others. Insights from neuroscience indicate that when we witness others experiencing emotions akin to our own, the very regions of our brain that ignite during our personal experiences also light up. This neural resonance facilitates our comprehension of others' thoughts, emotions, and sensations by mirroring them within ourselves. Emotion theories based on neurobiological research suggest that mirror neurons enable us to perceive and understand others' feelings without words, facilitating emotional understanding and resonance.

Challenges Faced by Empaths

Empaths, individuals with the unique ability to sense and absorb the feelings of others, possess a remarkable yet demanding gift. The article "14 Problems Only Empaths Will Understand" in *highlysensitiverefuge.com* sheds light on the struggles accompanying this heightened emotional sensitivity.

1. **Others' emotions can flip yours like a switch:**

Empaths often experience a sudden shift in emotions when they encounter the feelings of those around them. What might have been a good day can quickly turn sour when confronted with a friend or loved one's distress.

2. **You're constantly battling emotional fatigue:**

Empaths can experience overwhelming emotional fatigue from absorbing others' emotions and managing their own. This constant struggle necessitates diligent self-care practices to avoid exhaustion.

3. **Compassion can feel like a burden:**

While empathy is a cherished trait, empaths may feel burdened by their inability to switch off their compassion. This can result in carrying the emotional weight of others' suffering, often feeling responsible for remedying it.

4. **You're torn between going out and staying in:**

Empaths crave connection with others yet require ample alone time to recharge from the emotional energy they absorb. Striking a balance between socializing and solitude presents a continuous struggle for these individuals.

5. **Alone time is necessary — and not everyone understands that:**

Communicating the need for solitude can be challenging, especially when others fail to comprehend its vital role in an empath's well-being. Clear communication and understanding from loved ones are essential.

6. **You need time to process transitions:**

Empaths may struggle with transitioning between high-stimulus environments and low-stimulus settings, requiring time to process the accompanying emotions.

7. **You struggle with anxiety or depression:**

The heightened sensitivity of empaths leaves them vulnerable to experiencing a wide spectrum of mental health challenges, including anxiety and depression, as they absorb the emotions of those around them.

8. **You know someone is feeling "off" when no one else notices:**

Empaths possess an intuitive ability to sense others' emotional states, often detecting distress before it becomes apparent to others. While this is beneficial, it can interfere with their enjoyment in social settings.

9. **People take advantage of your compassion:**

Empaths' empathic intuition may attract individuals seeking to exploit their compassion. Setting boundaries and recognizing red flags is crucial for protecting their well-being.

10. "Small" things can deeply upset you:

Empaths care deeply about everything, making them susceptible to being deeply affected by seemingly insignificant events or interactions.

11. Sometimes, you forget to leave emotional space for yourself:

Balancing the listener, healer, and problem solver role can lead empaths to neglect their emotional needs. Prioritizing self-care is essential for maintaining emotional well-being.

12. Saying no is hard:

Empaths may struggle to assert boundaries and say no, fearing disappointment or causing hurt to others. Learning to prioritize their own needs is a crucial aspect of self-care for empaths.

13. Violence and horror deeply upset you:

Empaths find it challenging to detach from the emotional impact of violence or horror, often experiencing prolonged distress after exposure to such stimuli.

14. You don't always know which emotions are yours:

Constantly absorbing emotional information from others can blur the line between their emotions and those of others, making it difficult for empaths to discern their true feelings.

While being an empath offers a deep understanding of other's emotions, it also presents unique challenges that require careful navigation and self-awareness.

"Introverts probably have a higher degree of sensitivity to outside stimulus and tend to back off. In your quiet shyness as a child, you end up with an accumulation of thoughts and ideas, building up big, imaginative worlds. You have to get it all out somehow, so it goes into your work."- **Matt Bellamy.**

Experience of a Hyper Empath

The article "'I feel your pain': confessions of a hyper-empath" was written by Joanna Cannon and published by The Guardian. In the article, Cannon narrates her experiences as a hyper-empath, a term she uses to describe individuals who deeply feel and empathize with the emotions and experiences of others.

Cannon begins by recounting childhood experiences where she effortlessly absorbed accents and emotions from her surroundings. She describes how being a hyper-empath involves not just feeling one's own emotions intensely but also absorbing and experiencing the emotions of others, often to the point of overwhelming sensitivity.

Throughout the article, Cannon delves into the challenges of being a hyper-empath, including feeling emotionally drained by taking on the pain and suffering of others. She reflects on her time as a junior doctor, where her hyper-empathy made it difficult for her to separate her emotions from those of her patients, leading to emotional exhaustion and difficulty coping.

Despite the challenges, Cannon also highlights the positive aspects of being a hyper-empath, such as providing comfort and understanding to others and having a heightened intuition. She emphasizes the importance of finding balance and coping strategies to manage overwhelming emotions, suggesting practical steps like stepping back from emotionally taxing situations, rationalizing feelings, and engaging in self-care activities. Cannon concludes by sharing her journey of turning her empathy into a positive force, mainly through her writing. She suggests that being a hyper-empath isn't all about pain and misery but can also be a source of strength and connection with others.

The Neuroscience Behind Empathy

Understanding the Intricacies of Emotional Connection" is an illuminating article featured in the Association for Psychological Science, delving into the complex neural mechanisms that underpin empathy. Through interviews with five scientists at an Integrative Science Symposium, this article unravels the mysteries of empathy, shedding light on its neurological underpinnings, cultural influences, developmental aspects, and practical applications.

1. Christian Keysers, from the Netherlands Institute for Neuroscience, highlights how observing others' actions or emotions activates corresponding neural networks in the observer's brain, suggesting a mirroring effect.

2. Claus Lamm, from the University of Vienna, discusses experiments involving placebo painkillers, revealing a link between reduced self-experienced pain and decreased empathy for other's pain, as evidenced by changes in brain activity.

3. Ying-yi Hong, an APS Fellow from the Chinese University of Hong Kong, examines the influence of cultural factors on empathy. She demonstrates differences in brain responses to in-group versus out-group members and suggests that societal contexts play a significant role.

4. Rebecca Saxe, a researcher at the Massachusetts Institute of Technology (MIT), explores the development of empathy in children, identifying distinct brain networks involved in considering others' minds and bodies, even in infants as young as six months old.

5. Brian D. Knutson, from Stanford University, discusses neuro forecasting, linking brain activity in regions associated with gain anticipation and loss anticipation to individual choices. This offers

insights into consumer behavior and market dynamics.

These scientists' groundbreaking observations and research findings paint a vivid portrait of empathy as a fundamental aspect of human nature rooted in the intricate workings of the brain. This comprehensive exploration deepens our understanding of empathy and opens new avenues for harnessing its power to foster compassion, knowledge, and societal harmony.

Healing Strategies for Empaths

In her illuminating guide, "The Empath's Survival Guide," renowned psychiatrist Judith Orloff, M.D., offers invaluable insights and practical strategies for empaths to heal from trauma and thrive in their sensitive nature.

Orloff emphasizes that empaths and sensitive individuals often experience post-traumatic stress due to years of sensory overload and early experiences of neglect, abuse, or feeling unrecognized. Early trauma can manifest in various forms, from witnessing frequent arguments to experiencing emotional or physical abuse, leading to hypervigilance and a heightened sense of threat perception.

Healing Strategies:

1. **Journaling:** Orloff encourages empaths to write about their early traumas as a crucial first step towards awareness and healing, acknowledging that no trauma is too insignificant to address.

2. **Inner Child Retrieval:** Through visualization, empaths can reconnect with their wounded inner child, offering comfort, validation, and reassurance that they are safe and loved.

3. **Emotional Release:** Allowing oneself to feel and express emotions such as anger, fear, and self-doubt is essential for healing. Orloff recommends seeking support from a therapist to create a safe space for emotional processing.

4. **Setting Boundaries:** Empaths must learn to assert themselves and establish clear boundaries to protect their emotional well-being. Saying "no" when necessary and assertive communication are vital skills to cultivate.

5. **Conscious Breathing:** When triggered by past traumas, empaths can practice deep breathing to calm their nervous system and regain composure before responding.

6. **Meditation:** Regular meditation helps empaths quiet their minds, reduce sensory overload, and maintain inner peace amidst external challenges.

7. **Self-Compassion:** Orloff emphasizes the importance of showering oneself with love and kindness throughout the healing journey, recognizing that self-compassion is a fundamental aspect of self-care.

Orloff suggests consulting a therapist trained in trauma-focused techniques such as EMDR or Emotional Freedom Tapping to address deep-seated trauma effectively. Additionally, incorporating somatic awareness practices and holistic therapies like massage or energy work can aid in releasing residual trauma stored in the body.

By embracing these healing strategies, empaths can gradually overcome past traumas, strengthen their empathic abilities, and create a sense of safety and peace. With patience, self-love, and a commitment to healing, empaths can transform their lives and navigate the world with resilience and authenticity.

Orloff encourages empaths to acknowledge their early traumas, recognize patterns in their current relationships, and affirm their capacity for healing. Through intentional self-care and compassion, empaths can embark on a transformative journey toward wholeness and empowerment.

Judith Orloff, M.D., offers hope and guidance for empaths seeking healing and self-empowerment. By honoring their experiences, embracing self-care practices, and seeking support, empaths can reclaim their inner strength and thrive amidst life's challenges.

Mapping Brilliance

Identify the challenges stemming from your sensitivity and employ healing strategies to address them.

3. Strength of Sensitivity

"Sensitive people get a bigger boost from the same things that help anyone: a mentor, a healthy home, a positive group of friends. This boost allows them to do more and go further if they are given a nudge in the right direction. Sensitive people are built for super growth."- Jenn Granneman, Andre Sólo.

Amidst the high stakes of Australia's 2019 World Cup campaign, star all-rounder Glenn Maxwell faced a personal battle away from the public eye. Despite his success on the field, Maxwell was silently struggling with anxiety and despair.

Maxwell experienced a pivotal moment during a routine practice session prior to a crucial match against South Africa when he was struck on the arm. Although the injury wasn't severe, it served as a catalyst for Maxwell to confront his deeper feelings and desires. In a candid admission, Maxwell revealed that amidst his frustration, a part of him harbored a hidden wish for a more significant break from the relentless demands of international cricket.

This incident marked a turning point for Maxwell as he recognized the importance of acknowledging his mental well-being amidst the pressures of elite sports. His decision to openly address his struggles and take a temporary hiatus from cricket showcased his courage and commitment to prioritizing his mental health. Maxwell's journey underscores the complexities and challenges athletes face in managing their psychological wellness within the competitive world of professional sports.

Maxwell's difficulties persisted as the tournament advanced, culminating in Australia's defeat to England in the semi-finals. Despite his contributions in the final game, Maxwell found little comfort in his performance, with his mental health continuing to suffer.

However, things took a remarkable turn at the 2023 World Cup. Maxwell scored an awe-inspiring 201* against Afghanistan in an extraordinary display of skill and resilience. Cricket icon Sachin Tendulkar joined the chorus of praise for Maxwell's innings, lauding it as an unparalleled ODI performance in his experience. This recognition added a profound layer to Maxwell's journey, highlighting his exceptional talent and the indomitable spirit of an athlete overcoming personal adversity. Maxwell's return was undoubtedly a cause for celebration, but what truly stands out is his bravery in embracing vulnerability to articulate his genuine feelings and the necessity for a respite, shedding light on his mental health journey.

A nuanced approach to nurturing marks the journey of sensitivity from a perceived weakness to a tangible strength. Embracing sensitivity as a gift is indispensable, as it promises to foster positive societal change. Courage plays a pivotal role in articulating truths. Authenticity and vulnerability serve as the driving force behind this transformation, elevating sensitivity to a position of influence and impact.

"Vulnerability is the birthplace of innovation, creativity, and change." - **Brené Brown.**

Imagine living in an era when sensitivity was widely misunderstood, which caused the struggles faced by those individuals to go largely unrecognized. Today, we benefit from literature and social media platforms that shed light on various personality types and their traits, empowering us with greater understanding and acceptance. Thanks to the bravery of those who dared to share their inner worlds, we now live in a more enlightened age surrounded by an educated and empathetic community.

Strength of Sensitivity

In a TIME magazine article by Andre Sólo titled "Why Being Sensitive Is a Strength," sensitivity is reframed as a powerful asset rather than a weakness. Sólo, known for his work with *Sensitive Refuge*, the world's largest website for sensitive individuals, challenges sensitivity misconceptions. While society often perceives sensitivity as a liability associated with fragility and overreaction, Sólo argues that it's an innate trait, profoundly ingrained and predominantly genetic.

Research spanning three decades suggests that sensitive individuals process information more deeply, leading to heightened creativity, empathy, and critical thinking. They excel in detail-oriented tasks and problem-solving, often contributing to innovation and caregiving roles. Moreover, sensitive individuals usually experience what Sólo calls the "Boost Effect," deriving more significant benefits from training and support than their less-sensitive counterparts. This heightened cognitive ability allows them to thrive with proper support and training.

Despite societal pressures to suppress sensitivity, Sólo encourages individuals to embrace it, emphasizing its unique advantages. However, sensitivity also poses challenges, such as overstimulation in chaotic environments. Yet, sensitive individuals can effectively manage these challenges through self-awareness, setting boundaries, and seeking support.

By nurturing empathy and compassion, they forge deeper connections and positively impact those around them. Ultimately, embracing sensitivity enables individuals to unlock their full potential and make meaningful contributions personally and professionally. In a world where sensitivity is increasingly recognized as vital for innovation and interpersonal relationships, fostering supportive environments becomes essential for individuals and organizations.

Vantage Sensitivity

Vantage sensitivity, a concept elucidated by Michael Pluess and Jay Belsky, delves into the varied responses individuals exhibit towards positive experiences and nurturing environments. This framework underscores the notion that certain people tend to derive greater benefits from supportive factors like parental nurturing, positive relationships, and psychological interventions, while others may not exhibit the same degree of responsiveness, or perhaps none at all.

This concept contrasts with vantage resistance, where individuals fail to benefit from positive experiences due to the absence of factors that facilitate sensitivity. It's theorized that various factors, including genetic, physiological, and psychological traits, influence vantage sensitivity. For instance, genetic studies have shown that specific gene variants are associated with heightened sensitivity to positive experiences. At the same time, physiological markers like cortisol reactivity indicate a more robust positive response to supportive influences.

Psychologically, individuals who score high on sensitivity measures tend to respond more positively to interventions and environmental changes. Studies have demonstrated that highly sensitive individuals, particularly children, are more likely to benefit from psychological interventions and positive school environments. High sensitivity predicts a more significant response to positive stimuli and improved adult task performance.

Vantage sensitivity illuminates how individuals interact with their environments and underscores the importance of understanding these individual differences in designing interventions and fostering positive environments for optimal development and well-being.

Strategies to Strengthen Sensitivity

Sensitive people must be skilled at navigating and excelling in a world not necessarily designed for their unique traits. In today's fast-paced society, constant connectivity and overwhelming information overload are the norms. Michael Pluess's work reveals that HSPs flourish in nurturing environments. To harness this potential for success, HSPs must cultivate specific skills.

Here are several impactful strategies individuals can embrace, gleaned from the valuable insights shared in the article 'The Eight Secret Skills That Will Help You Thrive as a Highly Sensitive Person' on highlysensitiverefuge.com. These approaches offer practical guidance for individuals seeking to navigate their high sensitivity with resilience and confidence. These strategies offer valuable guidance for navigating the unique challenges and maximizing the strengths associated with high sensitivity.

1. **Mindfulness:** Developing a consistent mindfulness practice is essential for HSPs to manage and prevent emotional overload. By

cultivating awareness of thoughts, sensations, and breath control, HSPs can effectively regulate their emotions.

2. **Rewriting Limiting Beliefs:** Recognizing and challenging misconceptions about sensitivity is crucial. HSPs should embrace their innate strengths, such as intuition, empathy, and creativity, instead of viewing sensitivity as a weakness.

3. **Setting Healthy Boundaries:** Maintaining energy levels and preventing overwhelm requires setting healthy boundaries. HSPs must learn to discern when to say "yes" and when to prioritize self-care.

4. **Self-Compassion:** Practicing self-compassion is vital for HSPs to combat inner criticism and perfectionism. By acknowledging mistakes and prioritizing self-care, HSPs can reduce anxiety and stress levels.

5. **Effective Communication:** Expressing feelings and needs to others, using tools like Non-Violent Communication, is essential for HSPs to maintain healthy relationships while honoring their unique needs.

6. **Building Awareness of Values:** Identifying and aligning with personal values allows HSPs to make decisions contributing to fulfillment and well-being.

7. **Engaging in Grounding Rituals:** Connecting with something beyond the ego, whether through meditation, yoga, or nature, helps HSPs reduce anxiety and stress, fostering relaxation and connection.

8. **Authenticity and Integration:** Embracing all aspects of oneself, including hidden or suppressed traits, leads to healing and wholeness. HSPs thrive when they honor their authenticity and integrate the shadow parts of their identity.

9. **An Avenue for Expression:** Sensitive individuals can satisfy their expression needs by engaging in various artistic pursuits, such as visual arts, media creation, podcasts, or writing. By immersing themselves in these creative outlets, they can nurture their cognitive growth through exploration and self-expression.

10. **Guided by Supportive Environments:** Engaging with goal-oriented communities or receiving mentorship can unlock the full potential of sensitive individuals.

With these strategies, HSPs can navigate challenges effectively, harness their unique strengths, and lead fulfilling lives in a world that often overlooks their needs and contributions.

How Sensitivity is Brilliance?

In today's world, sensitivity often faces stigma and undervaluation. Yet, a deeper examination reveals a compelling intersection between sensitivity and brilliance, challenging stereotypes and accentuating the strengths of sensitive individuals. Research by Linda Silverman suggests a correlation between high IQ and sensitivity, indicating that gifted individuals frequently exhibit sensitive traits. The concept of overexcitability, particularly emotional overexcitability, sheds further light on this connection. Sensitivity emerges not as a weakness but a valuable trait linked to exceptional intelligence and talent.

Furthermore, insights on intuition shed additional light on the concept of brilliance. When coupled with intellect, intuition is a significant factor in decision-making processes. Contrary to popular belief, intuition does not solely rely on gut feelings but involves discerning irrelevant information that can be discarded. Disciplined intuition emphasizes the importance of thorough research in enhancing intuitive abilities and complementing rationality in decision-making.

In leadership contexts, the importance of vulnerability is underscored. Vulnerability can act as a catalyst for trust and authenticity. Leaders can foster supportive environments where vulnerability is celebrated through personal storytelling, accountability, empathy, open communication, and active listening. This approach offers actionable insights for leaders to embrace vulnerability, fostering resilience and high performance in today's dynamic landscape.

Factors of Sensitivity Intelligence

Highly intelligent individuals possess a unique blend of qualities that set them apart. According to an article featured in the World Economic Forum, they exhibit remarkable adaptability, thriving in diverse environments by demonstrating resilience and ingenuity in the face of challenges. Coupled with a humble acknowledgment of their limitations, they embrace curiosity as a driving force, eagerly exploring the intricacies of the world around them. Their adeptness at asking insightful questions challenges existing paradigms and sparks innovative solutions to complex problems. Empathetic sensitivity characterizes their interactions, as they demonstrate a profound understanding of others' experiences and emotions. Remaining open-minded, they eagerly consider alternative viewpoints and solutions, fostering an environment conducive to creativity and growth. Yet, their discerning skepticism ensures a rational approach, withholding belief until presented with compelling evidence. These traits collectively define the essence of highly intelligent individuals, shaping their contributions to personal and societal advancement.

Sensitivity encompasses various facets of intelligence, including perceptiveness, emotional awareness, adaptability, empathy, creativity, and aesthetic appreciation. Recognizing sensitivity as a form of intelligence underscores its value in navigating and understanding the complexities of human experience and the world. Here are some factors discussed in *exploringyourmind.com* on why sensitivity can be considered a form of intelligence:

1. **Perceptive Observation**: Highly sensitive individuals are keen to observe and understand their surroundings, noticing intricate details and subtle cues that others may overlook. This acute awareness reflects a depth of intelligence in their perceptiveness.

2. **Adaptive Response to Feedback**: Sensitivity towards criticism indicates an individual's receptivity to external feedback, which, when handled constructively, fosters personal growth and development. This ability to adapt and learn from critique showcases emotional intelligence.

3. **Enhanced Environmental Awareness**: Highly sensitive individuals possess a heightened appreciation for their environments, attuned to nuances in sensory experiences such as colors, sounds, and smells. Their ability to navigate and respond to different environmental stimuli demonstrates a form of environmental intelligence.

4. **Empathetic Understanding:** Sensitivity is closely linked with empathy, as individuals attuned to their own emotions are often more adept at understanding and sharing the feelings of others. This empathetic capacity reflects a deep emotional intelligence and interpersonal awareness.

5. **Creative Imagination:** Sensitivity is associated with a rich imagination and creativity, enabling individuals to engage deeply with art, nature, and abstract concepts. This imaginative prowess is indicative of cognitive intelligence and inventive thinking.

6. **Connection to Aesthetic Intelligence:** Studies suggest a correlation between sensitivity and aesthetic appreciation, particularly among gifted individuals who demonstrate heightened sensitivity to beauty. This aesthetic intelligence encompasses a profound understanding and appreciation of artistic expression and cultural significance.

"The true sign of intelligence is not knowledge, but imagination."-**Albert Einstein.**

Steps for Sustaining Empathy

Understanding the nuances between empathic distress and empathic concern is essential, as empathy can serve as both a profound connection and a potential source of distress. Empathic distress, characterized by negative emotions, withdrawal, and burnout, contrasts with empathic concern, which cultivates positive feelings, good health, and a desire to aid others. Psychologists suggest the following steps to prevent being consumed by empathic distress.

1. Recognize signs of distress when empathizing with others.
2. Increase tolerance for emotions and embrace discomfort.
3. Practice conscious self-awareness to avoid the "empathy trap."
4. Visualize emotions as passing clouds and hold space for them without reacting.
5. Challenge negative interpretations of situations.
6. Engage in cognitive reappraisal to shift perspective and manage distress.
7. Exercise resilience by accepting emotions until they pass.
8. Recognize that you can't solve emotions like you solve problems.
9. Express emotions openly with trusted individuals.
10. Accept discomfort and communicate a willingness to support others.
11. Consider Non-Violent Communication (NVC) training for emotional expression.
12. Engage in compassion training to develop empathy and resilience.

13. Stay true to the narrative by understanding the other person's experience.
14. Practice mindfulness techniques like loving-kindness meditation.
15. Focus on understanding others' experiences without making it about oneself.
16. Express empathy without integrating personal experiences.
17. Use concise statements to convey support and understanding.
18. Respect and validate others' emotions without shifting focus to personal experiences.

Following these steps and techniques can help individuals develop and strengthen their empathy, enrich human interactions, and improve interpersonal relationships. It empowers individuals to become more empathic listeners and fosters a more empathetic society.

Mapping Brilliance

List out your sensitivity strengthening and preservation areas and apply the techniques mentioned.

4. Practical Empathy

"Empathy has no script. There is no right way or wrong way to do it. It's simply listening, holding space, withholding judgment, emotionally connecting, and communicating that incredibly healing message of 'You're not alone.'"- Brene Brown.

Mahatma Gandhi often found himself hurrying from one place to another. On one particularly hectic day, he was racing against time to catch a train. Gandhi dashed along the platform and vaulted into the third-class compartment he customarily traveled in as the locomotive chugged out of the station. Helpful hands reached out to pull him aboard, but one of his sandals slipped off in the commotion and fell to the ground. As the train continued, a chorus of disappointed sighs emanated from the onlookers, marking the departure of Gandhi's lone sandal, abandoned on the platform. Gandhi leaned over, swiftly removed his remaining sandal without hesitation, and tossed it back onto the tracks. Bystanders, puzzled by his action, inquired, "Mahatma, why discard your other sandal?" With a gentle smile, Gandhi responded, "The person who finds the first sandal might as well have the second. It would be of greater use as a pair."

Gandhi's action exemplified practical empathy. Recognizing that the sandal would be more useful in pairs, he acted within his capacity to ensure whoever found it would benefit fully. This simple act reflects Gandhi's ability to consider others' perspectives and demonstrates his commitment.

Empathy thrives in sensitive individuals who often feel more deeply than others. This innate ability is a valuable skill, particularly beneficial in mediation, inclusion, innovation, creativity, and counseling.

"When you show deep empathy toward others, their defensive energy goes down, and positive energy replaces it. That's when you can get more creative in solving problems."- **Stephen Covey.**

Practical empathy

Practical empathy goes beyond simply understanding and sharing the feelings of others; it involves leveraging this understanding to drive action and solutions. It's about more than just experiencing someone else's emotions—it's about utilizing that insight to make decisions and effectively address their needs and concerns.

Practical empathy, a robust approach focused on understanding individuals' needs and backed by action, is highlighted in the 2024 Global Culture Report by O.C. Tanner. While empathy is widely recognized, its application in the workplace has often been challenging. However, practical empathy offers a potent, less burdensome, actionable solution. It fosters a sense of belonging and connection and yields tangible business benefits such as talent attraction and retention. The report emphasizes the necessity of coupling empathy with action for true impact, outlining six active components: focusing on the person, seeking understanding, active listening, embracing perspectives, taking supportive action, and respecting boundaries. It underscores the importance of leaders and organizations championing empathy as a practice and providing tools and support for effective action. Ultimately, practical empathy aims to build solid and meaningful connections in the workplace, prioritizing understanding and decisive action to create environments where employees feel valued, supported, and empowered.

The Advantages of Highly Sensitive People in the Workplace

Highly sensitive individuals possess unique strengths that make them valuable assets in the workplace, as outlined by Melody Wilding, LMSW, in *psychologytoday.com*. Managers consistently rate individuals with higher sensitivity as top contributors, indicating the significance of their innate qualities. Here are the advantages that highly sensitive people (HSPs) bring to the workplace:

1. Diplomacy: HSPs think deeply before speaking, allowing them to balance different perspectives and communicate tactfully, even under pressure.

2. Critical Thinking: With more active brain circuitry, HSPs process information profoundly and explore various angles of work challenges.

3. Self-awareness: HSPs possess unmatched self-awareness, enhancing their performance and adaptability in various work situations.

4. Innovation: Vigilant HSPs constantly seek improvements and identify gaps, contributing to creative problem-solving and innovation.

5. Information Management: HSPs excel in roles requiring organization, collaboration, and information management due to their depth of processing and conscientiousness.

6. Team Morale: HSPs' heightened empathy enables them to sense and respond to team morale, fostering a positive work environment.

7. Intuition: HSPs leverage their strong intuition and pattern recognition skills in decision-making, often outperforming non-HSPs in crisis management.

8. Thoroughness: Known for their dedication and professionalism, HSPs impress with their comprehensive preparation and commitment to excellence.

9. Focus on the Big Picture: HSPs drive towards larger purposes, helping teams stay focused and grounded amidst uncertainty.

10. Harmonious Work Environment: Passionate about inclusion, HSPs create environments where diverse working styles are valued, fostering collaboration and productivity.
11. Integrity: HSPs uphold fairness and integrity, speaking up against inequity and earning trust as reliable team members.
12. Continuous Growth: HSPs demonstrate a high personal and professional growth drive, ensuring ongoing career advancement.

Embracing the unique strengths of highly sensitive individuals enhances workplace dynamics and contributes to overall success.

Empathy varies among individuals, ranging from an instinct for some to a conscious effort for others, with some individuals lacking it entirely. Researchers have extensively studied, misunderstood, understood, defined, and redefined empathy over time. While some people exhibit empathy reflexively, others develop it through cognitive processes, while some may never fully embody it.

Empathy in Business

In a Harvard Business Review article by Jamil Zaki, the research underscores the benefits of empathic workplaces, including more vital collaboration, reduced stress, higher morale, and faster recovery from challenges like layoffs. Despite these advantages, many leaders struggle to instill empathy in their organizational culture. Zaki suggests leveraging appropriate social norms as a key strategy. The initial step is acknowledging that empathy can be developed rather than being an inherent trait. When empathy is viewed as something fixed, individuals may feel it's beyond their reach. Leaders should also be wary of "phantom norms," where a few outspoken individuals dominate behaviors, overshadowing the empathetic majority. Organizations can amplify empathy as a positive norm by highlighting empathy through incentives and recognition. Additionally, identifying connectors— individuals who foster team cohesion informally—and enlisting them to advocate for empathy can solidify its importance. This increases the likelihood of empathy becoming ingrained in the culture and allows employees to be acknowledged for connecting with others, reinforcing another positive social norm.

Cultivating Empathy: Insights from APA

In today's society, characterized by growing divisions, empathy emerges as a crucial trait for fostering kindness, cooperation, and tolerance towards others. Psychologists emphasize that empathy is a psychological "superglue," connecting individuals and promoting collaboration and kindness. Fortunately, research suggests empathy can be cultivated, offering hope for societal improvement.

Empathy drives various prosocial behaviors, such as volunteering, forgiveness, and helping others while reducing aggression and bullying. It motivates individuals to assist those in need and predicts charitable donation behavior. Moreover, empathy promotes better relationships and understanding among strangers and can help mitigate bias and systemic issues like racism.

However, not all forms of empathy are equally beneficial. While self-oriented perspective-taking, which involves imagining oneself in another's shoes, can lead to personal distress and hinder prosocial behaviors, other-oriented perspective-taking fosters compassion and empathy. This cognitive style consists of understanding another person's perspective without overidentifying with their emotions.

To cultivate empathy effectively, individuals can adopt several strategies:

1. **Adopting a Growth Mindset**: Believing in one's capacity to grow in empathy encourages more significant effort and empathy development.

2. **Exposure to Differences**: Immersing oneself in diverse experiences, cultures, and media content can broaden perspectives and enhance empathy.

3. **Engaging with Fiction**: Reading fiction and character-driven stories can improve understanding of others' experiences and emotions, fostering empathy.

4. **Harnessing Oxytocin**: Promoting oxytocin release through behaviors like eye contact and soft touch can facilitate empathetic responses and connection.

5. **Identifying Common Ground**: Finding shared identities or experiences with others can enhance empathy and motivate prosocial behaviors.

6. **Asking Questions**: Demonstrating curiosity and actively appreciating someone's perspective can deepen understanding and empathy.

7. **Understanding Empathy Blocks**: Recognizing personal barriers to empathy and actively addressing them can facilitate a more significant connection with others.

8. **Second-Guessing Assumptions**: By staying mindful of automatic judgments and exploring alternative perspectives, individuals can foster empathy and deepen understanding, particularly in difficult situations.

By embracing these strategies and approaches, individuals can cultivate empathy, contributing to a more compassionate and connected society.

Simon Sinek exemplifies the transformative impact of empathy through a dialogue scenario. He illustrates this by presenting two contrasting interactions. In the first scenario, an employee receives a stark performance review: "Your numbers are down for the fourth quarter. I don't know what will happen if it doesn't improve." However, empathy is infused into the conversation in the second scenario: "Your numbers are down for the fourth quarter; we have spoken about this before. I am worried about you.

Are you OK? What happened?" Sinek underscores that when individuals feel genuinely cared for and treated as human beings rather than mere statistics, they are inclined to invest their dedication and effort over the long term. He extends this principle to client relationships, advocating for a deeper understanding of clients beyond their financial status. By acknowledging their fears and aspirations, businesses can foster stronger connections and drive sustained success.

Exercises to Build Empathy

TED's "How to Be a Better Human" series features insights from various TED community members. It delves into the concept of empathy, highlighting its significance in understanding the emotions of others and its potential for development as a skill rather than a fixed trait. Stanford psychology professor Jamil Zaki emphasizes the benefits of empathy, not only for those receiving it but also for the empathizers themselves. He offers five exercises to enhance empathy, ranging from reflective practices to engaging with others in constructive dialogue and utilizing technology for meaningful connections.

Exercise #1: Strengthen your internal resources

This exercise involves reflecting on your struggles and how you respond to them. Then, imagine a friend experiencing the same issue and consider how you would react to them with patience, generosity, and forgiveness. This exercise highlights the difference in kindness between how we treat others and ourselves, fostering self-compassion as a foundation for empathy.

Exercise #2: Feeling spent? Spend kindness on others.

During moments of stress or limited capacity, seek out chances to engage in small acts of kindness toward others. This could involve sending encouraging messages, offering assistance, or lending a hand to those in need. Despite feeling drained, engaging in these acts can energize and uplift us, demonstrating that happiness and well-being are not diminished by giving to others.

Exercise #3: Disagree without debating

Engage in conversations with individuals you disagree with, but instead of debating or arguing, share personal stories that led to your opinions and listen to their perspectives without judgment. This exercise aims to foster understanding and empathy across differences, showing that disagreement doesn't have to lead to hatred.

Exercise #4: Use technology to connect, not just to click and comment

Reflect on how you use technology, mainly social media and messaging apps, and aim to use them as tools for genuine human connection rather than mindless scrolling or passive engagement. This involves being intentional about digital interactions, prioritizing real-time conversations, and actively seeking to connect with others rather than merely observing or reacting to online content.

Exercise #5: Praise empathy in others

Develop a habit of acknowledging and praising empathetic behavior in others, whether in personal interactions or professional settings. By recognizing and highlighting acts of kindness and empathy, we contribute to a culture that values and encourages compassionate behavior, fostering a positive feedback loop where kindness becomes more prevalent.

Regular practice of these exercises is intended to assist individuals in nurturing empathy on a daily basis, fostering a culture of compassion and understanding within society over time.

Mapping Brilliance

Enumerate your practical empathy skills and apply the exercises to address any areas for improvement.

5. Building Influence

"When you start to develop your powers of empathy and imagination, the whole world opens up to you."-Susan Sarandon.

In 2009, Dave Carroll and his band traveled on United Airlines when they witnessed baggage handlers mishandling their instruments, severely damaging Dave's $3,500 Taylor guitar. Despite filing a complaint and attempting to seek compensation for the damage, United Airlines' customer service proved unresponsive and uncooperative. Frustrated by the ordeal, he decided to take matters into his own hands.

Dave penned a catchy, humorous, yet poignant song titled "United Breaks Guitars," chronicling his frustrating experience with the airline. The song resonated deeply with audiences globally, captivating them with its clever lyrics and irresistible melody. Leveraging the power of social media, he showcased his creativity by debuting a captivating music video on YouTube, igniting a viral sensation across the internet.

"United Breaks Guitars" became a global sensation, resonating with fellow musicians who empathized with Dave's plight and other users who were frustrated with the customer service. The song's success brought attention to the power of social media as a tool for consumer advocacy.

Further it prompted a significant shift in how companies approached customer service and shone new light on managing brand reputation in the digital age.

Dave Carroll's story didn't end with just one song. He created a trilogy of "United Breaks Guitars" songs, each further amplifying his message about the importance of customer experience and accountability. The impact of his melodic efforts extended beyond the music industry, leading to Dave's recognition as a leading voice in customer service advocacy and social media innovation.

His book, "United Breaks Guitars: The Power of One Voice in the Age of Social Media," published in 2012, further delves into his experience with United Airlines and explores the broader implications of his story for businesses and consumers alike. Through his music, writing, and public speaking engagements, Dave Carroll inspires others to recognize the power of their voice and the importance of holding companies accountable for their actions.

Creativity has the power to persuade and influence actions effectively. When sensitivity is expressed openly through writing or speaking, it becomes a potent strength.

"One of the criticisms I've faced over the years is that I'm not aggressive enough or assertive enough or maybe somehow because I'm empathetic, it means I'm weak. I totally rebel against that. I refuse to believe that you cannot be both compassionate and strong."- **Jacinda Ardern, 40th Prime Minister of New Zealand**

Importance of Your Ability to Influence People

Strengthening one's ability to influence others is essential for anyone aspiring for leadership roles. In an HBR article, Benjamin Laker and Charmi Patel emphasize the importance of understanding two primary forms of influence: transactional and transformational.

Transactional influence involves concrete, task-oriented interactions, often seen in hierarchical organizations. On the other hand, transformational influence focuses on inspiring and motivating others through empathy and vision.

To master the art of influence, individuals must cultivate emotional connections and rapport with their team members. Active listening, commitment to the team's success, and leading by example are crucial components of effective influence. Leaders should strive to build trust, demonstrate commitment, and provide recognition to foster a positive and motivational work environment.

Mastering transformational influence becomes increasingly important in today's evolving workplace, where hierarchical structures are making way for more collaborative and flat organizational models. Leaders prioritizing empathy, support, and transparency are better positioned to drive meaningful change and inspire their teams toward shared goals.

Ultimately, by building genuine connections, fostering open communication, and leading with integrity, individuals can strengthen their ability to influence others positively and effectively navigate the complexities of leadership in the modern workplace.

"Influence is our inner ability to lift people up to our perspective." – **Joseph Wong.**

What is Influence?

Influence, different from bossy commands, is about gently guiding others toward a change without using force or direct orders. It's the skill of convincing people to do something because they genuinely see the benefits, not because they're scared of punishment. Unlike commands that force obedience in order to avoid trouble, influence makes people understand and believe in their actions.

An influential person can make others want to do things by explaining why it's important and how it will benefit everyone involved. They don't force people but help them see the bigger picture and why it matters. Influencers don't just change actions; they change the way people think.

For example, let's say you own a shop and want your employees to be friendlier to customers. Contrary to making threats of dismissal from the job, an influencer would talk to employees about why being friendly is good both for the customer and the business. This would make employees genuinely want to be friendly, even when the boss isn't around.

Influence inspires others to do the right thing by showing them why it's critical instead of pushing people around. In a world of rules and orders, actual influence is about getting people to believe in something enough to want to be a part of it.

"We need a variety of input, influence, and voices. You cannot get all the answers to life and business from one person or from one source." – **Jim Rohn.**

The Seven Traits of Successful Influencers:

Successful influencers understand that taking action is essential for achieving success. However, they also recognize that their impact goes beyond mere actions; it's rooted in a unique blend of traits that inspire others to listen, believe, and follow. These traits not only facilitate short-term changes but also have the power to transform lives.

The Seven Influence Traits are inherent in everyone to varying degrees, shaping their potential to influence others. By understanding and enhancing these traits, individuals can maximize their influence and effect meaningful change in both personal and professional spheres.

Dr. Karen Keller's research has identified these Seven Influence Traits™ as pivotal factors determining one's level of influence. Each trait contributes to an individual's overall influence potential, with higher scores indicating more excellent influence capabilities. Moreover, these traits are not static; individuals can actively develop and refine them to unleash their full influence potential.

The journey of increasing influence should start from within, cultivating self-awareness and understanding. As Lao Tzu wisely said, "Knowing others is intelligence; knowing yourself is true wisdom. Mastering others is strength; mastering yourself is true power."

Now, let's explore the Seven Influence Traits:

1. **Confidence**: Having a resilient "whatever-it-takes" mindset, believing in oneself, and trusting one's abilities.

2. **Commitment**: Demonstrating unwavering dedication and determination to achieve specific goals, especially in the face of challenges.

3. **Courage**: Tackle difficult circumstances and individuals with strength and resilience without backing down.

4. **Passion**: Fueling success with genuine enthusiasm, eagerness, and a sincere spirit for one's pursuits.

5. **Empowering**: Supporting and sharing knowledge with peers while recognizing and rewarding their contributions.

6. **Trustworthiness**: Upholding honesty, integrity, and reliability, as trust forms the cornerstone of influence.

7. **Likability**: Creating positive attitudes and fostering camaraderie, aligning people towards common goals with warmth and positivity.

Mastering these traits empowers individuals to become more influential, effecting positive change not only in their own lives but also in the lives of those around them. Through continuous development and application of these traits, individuals can unlock their full potential to lead and inspire others.

The Influence Model

The Influence Model, crafted by Allan R. Cohen and David L. Bradford, offers a strategic framework for navigating influence dynamics without relying on formal authority. Initially featured in their book "Influence Without Authority" (2005), this model addresses the limitations and drawbacks of traditional hierarchical power structures. Cohen and Bradford challenge the notion that authority guarantees cooperation and commitment. Instead, they advocate for a more nuanced approach that leverages reciprocal relationships and mutual understanding. The foundation of the Influence Model rests on the principle of reciprocity—the belief that positive actions toward others will be reciprocated over time.

Utilizing the Influence Model becomes essential when traditional authority is insufficient or ineffective. It proves particularly valuable when seeking assistance from individuals who may initially resist cooperation or in situations lacking rapport.

The model comprises six sequential steps:

1. **Assume Everyone Can Help You**: Adopting a mindset that perceives others as potential allies rather than adversaries sets the stage for collaborative influence.

2. **Prioritize Objectives**: Clarifying and aligning your goals with organizational objectives helps maintain focus and avoid personal biases that could impede negotiation.

3. **Understand the Other Person's Situation**: Delving into the circumstances and motivations of the individual you seek to influence enables you to tailor your approach effectively. Factors such as performance metrics, responsibilities, and organizational culture are crucial in understanding their perspective.

4. **Identify What Matters to You and to Them**: Recognizing and aligning with the other party's values and priorities forms the cornerstone of successful influence. Cohen and Bradford identify five categories of factors—inspiration, task, position, relationship, and personal—that are commonly valued in organizational contexts.

5. **Analyze the Relationship**: Assessing the quality and nature of your relationship with the individual

helps determine the most appropriate approach for influencing them. Building trust and rapport may be necessary before proceeding with negotiation or request.

6. **Make the "Exchange"**: Crafting a mutually beneficial exchange based on identified needs and priorities facilitates collaboration and fosters goodwill. By offering something of value in return for cooperation, you reinforce the principle of reciprocity and strengthen the relationship.

Through a practical example, we can illustrate the application of the Influence Model in real-life scenarios, such as navigating cross-functional collaboration or seeking support from colleagues. Mark, an accountant, is in need of assistance from Rob on a software issue. Noting Rob's heavy workload, Mark proposes a mutual exchange: he offers Rob a day's assistance in return for his time and expertise. Rob agrees, and their successful collaboration resolves the issue while strengthening their relationship.

By internalizing and implementing the steps outlined in the Influence Model, individuals can enhance their ability to influence others effectively, even in situations devoid of formal authority. This strategic approach not only facilitates cooperation and collaboration but also fosters a culture of reciprocity and mutual support within organizations.

"Courage gives us a voice, and compassion gives us an ear. Without both, there is no opportunity for empathy and connection." - **Brene Brown.**

Principles of Persuasion

Power represents the capacity of individuals to instigate change or exercise control over situations, events, and people. Frequently bestowed through official titles or positions, power is overt and conspicuous to others. In contrast, influence operates in ways more nuanced and, at times, indistinguishable. It is the aptitude to guide others towards adopting your perspective, not through direct control as seen in power, but through persuasive efforts that shape their perception of a situation or concept. The exercise of power often results in compliance, even if it is reluctant. Conversely, employing influence tends to garner consent, whether conscious or unconscious.

These principles, elucidated by Dr. Robert Cialdini, underpin effective persuasion strategies and influence behaviors across various contexts.

1. Reciprocation: People feel obliged to return favors, benefits, or positive actions. Giving first creates a sense of indebtedness, increasing the likelihood of receiving cooperation in return.

2. Liking: People are more inclined to comply with requests from those they like. Establishing similarities and offering genuine compliments can enhance rapport and foster positive relationships.

3. Social Proof: People often mirror the behaviors of those who resemble them, particularly when these individuals exhibit popularity or align with current trends. This demonstration of social validation can significantly sway decision-making processes.

4. Authority: People are more likely to follow the guidance of genuine experts. Associating ideas with credible authorities through testimonials or endorsements enhances persuasive impact.

5. Commitment and Consistency: Individuals strive to maintain consistency with their past commitments and actions, especially those made publicly. Aligning requests with existing commitments increases compliance.

6. Scarcity: People value items or opportunities more when they perceive them as rare or limited in availability. Highlighting scarcity or uniqueness can drive desire and urgency.

7. Unity: Individuals are more inclined to agree with and support those they perceive as part of their group or community. Establishing oneself as "one of us" fosters cooperation and willingness to comply.

Mapping Brilliance

Compile a list of steps necessary to cultivate influence.

6. Effective Compassionate Actions

"You think effectiveness with people and efficiency with things."- Stephen R. Covey. "Efficiency is doing things right; effectiveness is doing the right things."- Peter F. Drucker. "The effectiveness of your work will never rise above your ability to lead and influence others."- John C. Maxwell.

Maria Conceicao's name echoes far beyond her physical stature of 5'5". She's not just an individual; she's a force of nature, embodying resilience, determination, and boundless compassion.

Born into poverty and abandoned by her birth mother, Maria's early life was fraught with hardship. Raised by a poor refugee woman among seven siblings, she faced the harsh realities of life from a young age. Yet, adversity didn't define her; it fueled her determination to make a difference.

Her journey to becoming a beacon of hope started unexpectedly during a layover in Dhaka, Bangladesh. Stepping outside the confines of an airplane, she was confronted with the stark reality of poverty—a reality she couldn't ignore. Determined to act, she made a promise to 101 families and 600 children living in the slums: She would lift them out of poverty.

This promise wasn't just a fleeting thought; it became her driving force. Maria embarked on a remarkable odyssey, breaking barriers that were thought impossible for someone of her background. Maria shattered stereotypes at every turn, from cleaning toilets as a stewardess to conquering Everest and traversing the North and South Poles.

But her feats weren't for personal glory or fame; they were a means to an end. Maria knew education was the key to breaking the cycle of poverty. To fund the education of the children she promised to help, she turned to Guinness World Records, pushing her body to the limit in ultra-marathons and triathlons.

In Maria's journey, we find a potent reminder that our most significant achievements often stem from the simplest of promises. She teaches us that no dream is too audacious and no obstacle too daunting. Maria Conceicao isn't just a philanthropist or a motivational speaker; she's a testament to the indomitable spirit of the human heart. Her narrative will persist as a wellspring of inspiration for future generations, serving as a poignant reminder that through our collective efforts, we possess the capacity to impact lives positively, one commitment at a time.

"Compassion is not a virtue – it is a commitment. It's not something we have or don't have – it's something we choose to practice."- **Brené Brown.**

Committing to compassion and empathic actions isn't just for others; it's for yourself, too. Research shows these behaviors activate regions of the brain tied to pleasure and reward, producing positive psychological and physiological effects. This promotes overall well-being by fostering satisfaction and fulfillment.

Neuroscience of taking empathic action

In the discussion about purposeful empathy and the neuroscience behind empathic action, Dr. Lisa Aziz-Zadeh elaborates on the distinctions between sympathy, empathy, and compassion. Sympathy involves cognitively understanding someone's perspective, while empathy entails emotional resonance or sharing the feelings of others. On the other hand, compassion goes beyond understanding and consists in acting to help someone, activating reward circuits in the brain.

Dr. Aziz-Zadeh further explains the neural differences between these three states, highlighting the involvement of different brain regions for each state. Cognitive empathy or sympathy engages the prefrontal cortex and temporal parietal junction, while affective empathy or emotional resonance involves emotion-related brain regions like the insula. Compassion, however, activates reward circuits such as the basal ganglia and dopaminergic pathways. She explains the effects of empathy and compassion on the brain's pleasure and reward centers, emphasizing the importance of cultivating compassionate habits.

Compassion operates as a reciprocal reward system. Being compassionate brings happiness to others and generates happiness for yourself. Similarly, treating ourselves with kindness enables us to extend that kindness to others, forming a vital loop of empathy and self-care.

"We can't practice compassion with other people if we can't treat ourselves kindly." "If we can share our story with someone who responds with empathy and understanding, shame can't survive."- **Brene Brown.**

Shame is the root cause of personality disorders such as narcissism. An empathic atmosphere can influence vulnerability in people, helping to avoid stressful experiences and traumas. Developing courage and authenticity will help in avoiding becoming victims of such disorders.

Overcoming Empathy Challenges

The role of empathy has garnered significant attention in leadership development. However, Christine Comaford, drawing from her expertise in leadership coaching and neuroscience, challenges the notion that empathy alone is sufficient for navigating the complexities of modern interpersonal dynamics. Comaford promotes a thorough exploration of empathy and compassion, stressing the proactive nature of compassion in responding to the suffering of others.

Comaford's insights highlight empathy's potential pitfalls, such as biases, emotional burdens, and susceptibility to emotional residue. Paul Bloom's research further illuminates these challenges, underscoring empathy's tendency to foster tribalism and hinder objective decision-making. In response, Comaford promotes compassion as a superior alternative characterized by meaningful action and inclusivity.

Navigating this transition requires practical strategies for cultivating compassion in professional settings, including developing emotional intelligence and boundary-setting techniques. By fostering a culture of compassion, leaders can effectively address interpersonal challenges while promoting resilience and inclusivity within their teams.

Additionally, Mark Travers delves into the unique experiences of individuals identified as empaths, reframing their struggles with heightened empathy as opportunities for personal growth. Through leveraging neuroscience insights, empaths can harness their empathic abilities to deepen connections and facilitate positive change.

Lindsay Kohler further explores the practical implications of empathy in leadership, offering actionable insights for navigating its complexities effectively. From addressing similarity bias to understanding the limitations of focus groups, leaders can prioritize rational compassion over instinctual empathy to promote the greater good.

Dr. Aziz-Zadeh's research underscores the transformative impact of empathic actions in fostering social cohesion and reducing dehumanization. By exposing individuals to diverse social groups and instilling empathy through purposeful compassion training, leaders play a pivotal role in nurturing a world characterized by kindness and compassion.

Choosing Rational Compassion Over Empathy

Empathy is frequently hailed as a virtue essential for comprehending and forming deeper connections with others. However, Paul Bloom, a psychology professor at Yale University and the author of "Against Empathy: The Case for Rational Compassion," argues that empathy is a nuanced concept, challenging common perceptions of its role and significance.

Bloom suggests that empathy has the potential for good but is not inherently positive. He distinguishes between two interpretations of empathy: one as a broad concept of kindness and understanding and another as a narrower focus on comprehending others' experiences. While the latter is valuable, Bloom argues that it can also lead to adverse outcomes, especially when it favors individuals over collective well-being.

In exploring empathy, Bloom urges consideration of privilege. He highlights how empathy can be biased, with certain groups receiving more empathy than others due to systemic factors like racism and sexism. This imbalance, he argues, can perpetuate societal injustices.

To address these issues, Bloom proposes the concept of "rational compassion." Unlike empathy, which may prioritize individual experiences, rational compassion emphasizes the greater good of communities. It encourages a critical examination of biases and a focus on collective welfare.

In practical terms, practicing rational compassion requires awareness of biases and a commitment to accountability. For instance, empathy alone may not lead to meaningful action when confronting issues like climate change. Instead, rational compassion prompts us to consider the broader impact and advocate for systemic change.

Ultimately, Bloom's perspective suggests that while empathy has its place, it must be complemented by rational compassion to effect positive change. By integrating empathy and rational compassion into our interactions and decision-making processes, we can better understand others while prioritizing society's well-being. Choosing rational compassion over empathy challenges us to move beyond individual perspectives and embrace a broader, more inclusive approach to empathy and care. By doing so, we can work towards a more just and compassionate society.

People with compassionate empathy possess distinct characteristics that set them apart in their interactions and relationships. As described by Daniel Goleman, this form of empathy extends beyond merely understanding another's pain to being moved to alleviate it. Here's a closer look at the traits commonly associated with individuals who exhibit compassionate empathy:

1. **Balanced and Adaptive Response:** People with compassionate empathy have honed their ability to navigate various social situations with poise and sensitivity. They balance logic and emotion, allowing them to assess circumstances from a well-rounded perspective. Rather than being swayed solely by others' feelings or remaining detached in a purely logical mindset, they find a middle ground that enables them to offer meaningful support.

2. **Reciprocity:** Understanding the importance of reciprocity in relationships, individuals with compassionate empathy embody a spirit of mutual support and understanding. They offer assistance and empathy to others, recognize their needs, and deserve similar support in return. This reciprocity fosters healthy, nurturing relationships built on trust and mutual care.

3. **Mastery of Human Connection:** Compassionate empathy thrives on genuine human connection, characterized by authentic understanding and acceptance. These individuals approach others with sincerity, devoid of judgment or ulterior motives. They establish profound connections based on respect and appreciation by embracing each person's unique reality and needs.

Moreover, they possess the insight to discern unspoken needs and provide support effectively, even when not explicitly requested.

Strategies for Compassionate Actions

The HBR article "Connect with Empathy, But Lead with Compassion" by Rasmus Hougaard, Jacqueline Carter, and Marissa Afton is centered on the distinction between empathy and compassion in leadership roles. While empathy is crucial for understanding others' emotions, too much can overwhelm leaders and hinder their ability to make effective decisions. Conversely, compassion involves understanding and taking action to alleviate others' suffering without becoming emotionally entangled.

The article highlights the difference between empathy and compassion, emphasizing that while empathy involves feeling with the person, compassion entails understanding their experience and taking practical steps to help. It discusses the potential pitfalls of excessive empathy, such as clouded judgment and biased decision-making, citing research by Paul Bloom.

The article suggests several strategies for leaders to lead with compassion.

1. Taking a mental and emotional step away from the situation to gain perspective.
2. Asking individuals what they need allows them to reflect on their solutions.

3. Recognizing the power of non-action and simply being present to listen and acknowledge.

4. Coaching individuals to find their solutions rather than solving problems for them.

5. Practicing self-care to maintain emotional resilience and well-being.

The article underscores the importance of balancing empathy with rational compassion in leadership roles, enabling leaders to support others effectively while maintaining clarity and objectivity.

Effective Compassionate Actions: The Maria Conceicao Example

While simple empathy and kindness hold inherent value, rational compassion adds a strategic layer of thinking and objective analysis, ensuring that actions have the most significant impact and benefit for society. Below are the factors that make any action effective. Let's take Maria Conceicao's Example.

1. Addressing Root Causes: Maria addresses poverty's root cause by educating children.

2. Measurement of Impact/Data-based: She maintains her engagement with the children until they complete their education, providing tangible evidence of the positive outcomes stemming from her efforts.

3. Lasting/Permanent Solutions: Through education and empowerment, the children become self-

sufficient, no longer requiring ongoing support or intervention.

4. Goal-Based: Maria consistently works toward specific goals for the children in Bangladesh, ensuring her efforts are focused and purposeful.

5. Planned and system-based—not Random or Spontaneous: She meticulously plans her actions and leverages available resources, establishing a network of donors and sponsors to support her mission.

How impactful was Maria's effort to change the way those kids lived? She even trained herself to meet the ends. She was building influence when she ventured for marathons or to breaking Guinness records.

Effectiveness focuses on impacting many without bias but with total control within specified resources—a more inclusive approach. It will be more effective if a person chooses an area of action where their strength and interest lie, such that he can focus his energy on that area without needing external motivation.

"Give a man a fish and you feed him for a day; teach a man to fish and you feed him for a lifetime."- **Moses Maimonides.**

Mapping Brilliance

List compassionate actions you can initiate effectively by understanding and optimizing your unique strengths and weaknesses.

Conclusion

This book concludes the Fearless Empathy Series, crafted to Cultivate Empathy as Your Asset. Through meticulous research and extensive references across each volume, I aim to amass compelling evidence regarding the potential of intuitive feelers, or NF Personality types.

In this era of technological advancement and information abundance, we can access vast resources to enrich our comprehension and direction. Conversely, many predecessors lacked such fortune, yet those who did access pertinent information flourished, profoundly impacting lives. We can glean wisdom from their experiences to shape our paths.

Struggles are inherent to every generation, and it would be erroneous to claim ours as the most arduous. Despite challenges, we possess unprecedented technological support. However, the fundamental lessons for nurturing empathy remain consistent: Establish Boundaries, Master the Art of Saying No, Navigate Conflicts, Cultivate Resilience, Foster Connections, strive for a Balanced Personality, and harness your sensitivity as a strength. Embrace successful practices and frameworks, and foster connections within a nurturing environment—Dare, Share, and Celebrate.

GRAB YOUR FREE GIFT BOOK

MBTI enumerates 16 types of people in the world. Each of us is endowed with different talents, which prove to be the innate strength of our personality. To understand the deeper psychology of your personality type, unique cognitive functions, and integrated personality growth path, visit www.clearcareer.in for a free download –

"Your Personality Strength Report"

About the Author

Devi Sunny, a passionate author and mentor, has been fortunate to create the series: 'Clear Career Inclusive,' 'Fearless Empathy,' and 'Successful Intelligence.' She nurtures inclusive spaces, fosters empathetic leadership, and encourages cognitive growth. At Clear Career, she strives to offer guidance based on her experiences. If seeking supportive career insights, please reach out at contact@clearcareer.in

May I Ask for a Review

Thank you for taking out time to read this book. Reviews are the essential for any author. I look forward to your feedback and reviews for this book. I welcome your inputs to incorporate in and deliver an even better book in my next attempt in the very near future. Please write to me at:

contact@clearcareer.in

Your support will help me to reach out to more people. Thanks for supporting my work. I'd love to see your review and feel free to contact me for any clarifications.

Preview of Previous Books

Successful Intelligence Series

Book 1: Grow Practical Mindset

Are you prepared to elevate your adaptability, enhance practical problem-solving skills, and refine your judgment with practical intelligence?

Unlock the keys to practical intelligence with 'Grow Practical Mindset,' the inaugural book in the 'Successful Intelligence' series. Delve into the foundational principles of Sternberg's Triarchic Theory, focusing on adaptability and problem-solving skills crucial for success across diverse scenarios. *From practical exercises to insightful strategies, this book equips you with actionable tools to enhance decision-making in your daily life, empowering you to thrive in various environments.* This book will take you on an exhilarating journey through the following key topics, unraveling intriguing insights-

1. Practical Mindset
2. Triarchic Theory of Intelligence
3. Practical Intelligence
4. Examples of Practical Intelligence
5. 12 Traits for a Practical Mindset
6. Personality Types Natural Preferences
7. Cognitive Functions
8. Personality Growth
9. Fixed Mindset
10. How to Overcome a Fixed Mindset
11. Balancing Fixed and Growth Mindset
12. Growth Mindset
13. Right Environment
14. Courage Building
15. Mindset Growth Through Personality Awareness
16. Components and Strategies for Growth Mindset
17. The Growth Mindset: Examples for Practical Mindset of Idealists
18. What is Intelligent Thinking?
19. Types of Thinking
20. Cognitive Thinking Pattern of Idealists
21. Integrative Thinking

Elevate your adaptability and master the art of practical intelligence with this indispensable resource that offers tangible solutions and real-world applications.

Book 2: Grow Analytical Mindset

Are you seeking to sharpen your cognitive prowess, refine critical thinking, and unravel complex problems effortlessly through analytical intelligence?

Journey into the depths of cognition with 'Grow Analytical Mindset,' the second installment in the 'Successful Intelligence' series. Immerse yourself in Sternberg's Triarchic Theory, **exploring the nuances of analytical intelligence— refining critical thinking, problem-solving, and logical reasoning.** *Unlock expert strategies and exercises designed to sharpen your cognitive abilities, enabling you to dissect complexities easily.* This book will take you on an exhilarating journey through the following key topics, unraveling intriguing insights-

1. Analytical Mindset
2. Triarchic Theory of Intelligence
3. Analytical Intelligence
4. Applying Analytical Intelligence
5. Analytical Intelligence for Business Success
6. Personality Types and Cognitive Functions
7. System 1 and System 2 Thinking

Elevate your analytical prowess and confidently tackle challenges through this comprehensive guide.

Book 3 Grow Creative Mindset

Are you ready to awaken your creative genius, navigate uncharted territories, and craft innovative solutions by exploring inventive thinking and adaptability in problem-solving?

Embark on an enlightening journey with 'Grow Creative Mindset,' the third book in the 'Successful Intelligence' series. Delve into Sternberg's Triarchic Theory, exploring the depths of experiential intelligence, novelty creativity, and practical adaptation. *Unleash your innate creative potential through exercises and strategies designed to amplify your imaginative prowess, problem-solving finesse, and adaptability in ever-evolving scenarios.*

This book will take you on an exhilarating journey through the following key topics, unraveling intriguing insights-

1. Creative Mindset
2. Triarchic Theory of Intelligence
3. Creative Intelligence
4. Creative Thinking in Business
5. Personality Types and Cognitive Functions
6. Potential Environment of Creativity
7. Science Behind Creativity
8. Cognitive Functions of Idealists
9. Creative Personality Traits
10. Contradictory Traits of Creative Individuals
11. Enemy of Creativity
12. Are you a creative person?
13. Managerial Practices Affecting Creativity
14. Why We Struggle with Creativity
15. Minimalism for Creativity
16. Importance of Creativity in Business
17. Creativity at Workplace
18. AI-Enabled Automation and Creative Intelligence
19. Global Creativity Dynamics
20. Boosting Your Innovative Potential
21. Creativity and Design Thinking
22. Steps to Foster Creativity in Your Organization
23. 12 Types of Innovation Strategies
24. Ideation Process
25. 10 Effective Ideation Techniques
26. The transformative power of creative thinking
27. The Potential of Your Creativity
28. Qualification points for a good idea
29. Steps to Convert Ideas into Reality
30. Creativity and Successful Intelligence

Elevate your cognitive landscape and tap into the boundless realms of creativity with this transformative guide.

Fearless Empathy Series

Book 1 : Set Smart Boundaries

"Want to find the answers to the questions holding you back? *Ask yourself these five questions:*
1. Are you tired of feeling like a pushover in your personal and professional relationships? It's time to take control and set clear boundaries in the workplace.
2. Are you fed up with constantly giving in to others' demands and not standing up for yourself? Let's work on developing assertiveness skills in your personal and professional life.
3. Do you need help communicating your needs and wants confidently and effectively in your personal and professional life? Let's explore ways to improve your assertiveness.
4. Are you feeling drained and unappreciated in your personal and professional relationships? It may be time to take a hard look at how you set and enforce your boundaries.
5. Are you ready to take charge of your life and start living in alignment with your values in your personal and professional life? Let's work on building your assertiveness and boundary-setting skills.

"Set Smart Boundaries: is a comprehensive guide for anyone looking to improve their relationships, advance their career, and achieve their goals. **This book provides a specific, measurable, achievable, realistic, and time-bound approach to setting boundaries.** The natural ability to set boundaries is different for everyone. Certain people must consciously impose it as they cannot set boundaries naturally. In the MBTI 16Personality types, Intuitive & Sensory Feelers, require training in setting limits. Get ready for an eye-opening adventure as this book takes you on a journey through the subtopics below, unravelling intriguing insights and captivating stories.
1. Why Spot Takers?
2. Definition of Boundaries
3. Who should set boundaries?
4. How to spot takers?
5. Toxic behaviours in people.

This book is packed with practical advice, actionable tips, and real-life examples to help you set the boundaries you need to achieve success and happiness. Whether you're dealing with a demanding boss, a toxic friend, or a controlling partner, "Set Smart Boundaries" provides a step-by-step approach to help you take control of your life, career, and relationships.

Book 2 : Master Mindful No

Are you tired of feeling overwhelmed in a world that never stops demanding your attention?
Ask yourself these five questions:
1. Do you feel like you're constantly distracted and putting other people's needs ahead of your own, even if it means sacrificing your well-being? Let's Identify if you're a people pleaser and break free

from this habit, prioritizing your needs for a fulfilling life.
2. Do you struggle with being true to yourself and practicing self-care? Let's discover practical ways to practice real self-care and be more authentic for a more fulfilling life.
3. Are your fears holding you back from achieving your goals and living your best life? Let's explore your concerns and move forward with confidence and purpose.
4. Do you struggle with managing guilt and difficulties when you say "no"? Let's strategize for managing guilt and difficulties that may arise when speaking "no" to maintain healthy relationships and confidence.
5. Have you ever struggled with saying "no" without damaging your relationships or professional reputation? Let's Learn to say "no" positively and effectively, prioritizing our own needs while respecting the needs of others.

"Master Mindful No" offers practical strategies to help you filter distractions, overcome manipulation, and eliminate fear and guilt to succeed in a constantly demanding environment.
The natural ability to say No is different for everyone. Certain people must consciously learn it as they cannot be assertive naturally. In the MBTI 16Personality types, Intuitive & Sensory Feelers require training in prioritizing their needs.
This book takes you through the subtopics below, unraveling intriguing insights and captivating stories.
1. What is Mindfulness?
2. What is Mindful 'No'?
3. What is Distraction?
4. Why are we distracted?
5. Types of Distractions
6. Cost of Distraction
7. Practicing Mindful 'No' with Distractions
8. Root Causes of People Pleasing Behaviour
9. Courage Vs. Warmth
10. Manipulation Definition.
11. Signs of Manipulation
12. Practicing Mindful No with Manipulation.
13. What is Authenticity?
14. Authenticity and Sincerity

With practical exercises, real-life examples, and thought-provoking insights, "Master Mindful No" is the ultimate resource for anyone who wants to learn how to say "no" mindfully, with confidence and purpose. Whether you're struggling with people-pleasing tendencies or feeling overwhelmed by commitments, this book will help you navigate the complexities of modern life and live a more fulfilling, peaceful life.

Book 3: Conquer Key Conflicts

"Do you crave to break free from the relentless cycle of adjustment?"
Ask yourself these five pivotal questions:

1. Are you tired of avoiding conflicts and arguments and ready to develop the courage to face them head-on? Assess your growth values.
2. Are you seeking practical strategies to transform conflicts into opportunities? Uncover opportunities for success.

3. Do you want to understand the benefits of conflicts and learn how to manage them effectively? Navigate for positive outcomes.
4. Are you ready to choose healthy battles and leave your comfort zone? Discover more authentic answers.
5. Do you want constructive confrontation? Foster a positive attitude and deepen relationships.

"Conquer Key Conflicts" offers 7 **Effective Strategies** to Stop Avoiding Arguments, Develop the Courage to Disagree, and Achieve Deserving Results in a Challenging Environment.

The natural ability to face conflicts is different for everyone. Certain people must consciously learn it as they cannot be assertive naturally. In the MBTI 16Personality types, Intuitive & Sensory Feelers require training in prioritizing their needs. Discover a transformative guide to navigating conflicts with confidence and achieving excellent results. Explore the drawbacks of conflict avoidance, unlock the potential benefits of conflicts, and learn to choose healthy battles. This book takes you through the subtopics below, unraveling intriguing insights with examples.

1. Definition of Conflict
2. Triggers of Conflicts
3. Types of Conflict
4. Personality Types & Values
5. Values of MBTI Types
6. Personal Value Conflicts
7. What is Conflict Avoidance?
8. Signs of Conflict Avoidance
9. Conflict Avoidance or Value imbalance?
10. Values for growth
11. Result of Conflict Avoidance in Organisation.
12. Tips for Overcoming Conflict Avoidance
13. Should we encourage conflicts?
14. Disagreeing at work
15. Advantages of Conflicts at Work
16. Merits of Difficult Conversations
17. Conflict of Interest
18. Examples of Conflict of Interest at Work
19. Differentiating Conflicts
20. Arguments to Avoid
21. Choosing Value Conflicts for Success

From understanding the nature of disputes to **embracing healthy confrontation**, this book takes you on a journey of self-discovery and empowerment. *With practical strategies for resolution, you'll develop the courage to disagree and achieve positive outcomes in any challenging environment.*

Book 4: Build Emotional Resilience

Are you tired of being swept away by the chaos of life, losing your balance in the turbulence?
Ask yourself these five questions:
1. What if you could navigate life's challenges without being overwhelmed? Get ready to rewrite your relationship with adversity.
2. Have you ever felt your emotions spinning out of control? Dive into the heart of emotional imbalance and discover the tools to regain control.
3. What if you could break free from emotional dependence? Explore the empowering merits of emotional independence and learn how to cultivate it.
4. Can emotions indeed be your allies? Gain the power to make informed decisions and forge a more authentic path.
5. What if you could gracefully dance through life's ups and downs? Discover how to cultivate this invaluable skill and watch as life's challenges transform into opportunities for growth.
Step into emotional reinforcement, where you'll learn how to nurture and magnify the emotions that uplift you. This is your guide to mastering Emotional Resilience and thriving in

chaos. *With captivating stories, practical exercises, and eye-opening insights, this book is your companion on the journey to a calmer, more empowered you.*

The innate capacity to process emotions varies among individuals. Some people may need to consciously develop this skill, especially if they possess heightened sensitivity. According to the MBTI 16 Personality Types, individuals categorized as Intuitive and Sensory Feelers may benefit from acquiring Emotional Resilience through training. This book takes you through the subtopics below, unraveling intriguing insights and captivating stories.

1. Emotional Resilience
2. Emotional Intelligence Vs. Emotional Resilience
3. Factors Influencing Emotional Resilience
4. Negative Emotions
5. Emotional Setbacks
6. Relevance of Emotional Resilience
7. People Vulnerable to Frequent Emotional Imbalance
8. Highly Sensitive Persons (HSPs) and Empaths
9. Emotional Imbalance and Energy
10. Emotional Imbalance Based on Personality Type Cognitive Functions
11. Emotional Imbalance Based on Trauma
12. Emotional Independence
13. Ways to Achieve Emotional Independence
14. The Power of Detachment
15. The Power of Non-Reaction
16. Emotions are built, not built-in
17. Three Ways to Better Understand Your Emotions
18. Premeditatio Malorum
19. The Theory of Constructed Emotions
20. Strategies for Emotional Intelligence at Work
21. The Science of Romantic Love
22. Three Methods to manage emotions in the workplace
23. Habits of Emotionally Disciplined Leaders
24. Emotional Agility
25. Radical Acceptance of Emotions
26. Measuring Emotional Agility and Resilience
27. Emotional Agility for Workplace Success
28. Emotional Agility for Effective Leadership
29. Shame Resilience Therapy

This book unveils the intelligence hidden within your emotions and teaches you how to harness their wisdom. Emotional Resilience is your ticket to fluidly adapting to any situation.

Book 5: Develop Vital Connections

Are you weary of navigating the ruthless battleground of modern life without a safety net?
Ask yourself these pivotal questions:

1. What if you could harness the power of effective communication and self-expression to overcome life's challenges confidently? Understand the profound impact of connections on your growth, happiness, and success.
2. Have you ever considered the advantages of a robust support system in our competitive world? Discover the benefits of nurturing personal and professional relationships.
3. Struggling to establish vital connections? Learn to identify and conquer common barriers that hold you back.
4. How can you choose connections that elevate your life? Gain the wisdom to cultivate relationships that truly empower you.
5. Need techniques for lasting connections? Equip yourself with practical strategies to build meaningful bonds.

Step into vital connections, where you'll learn the art of mastering effective communication, empowering your self-expression, and enhancing your value in this competitive arena. *This book isn't just a guide; it's your steadfast companion on the journey toward a more connected, thriving you.*
Innate connection-making abilities differ among individuals.
Some may need to develop this skill, especially if they prefer

solitude consciously. According to MBTI's 16 Personality Types, Introverted Intuitives can benefit from strengthening their connection-building skills.
In a world where the ability to build and maintain vital connections is your golden ticket to success, whether you're a natural social butterfly or someone who could use a bit of extra guidance, **"Develop Vital Connections" reveals the intelligence concealed within the craft of connection-building, teaching you how to harness its incredible potential.**
This book will take you on an exhilarating journey through the following key topics, unraveling intriguing insights and sharing captivating stories:

1. Vital Connections
2. Attachment Styles
3. Factors of Connections for Growth
4. Effective Communication vs. Self Expression
5. The Power of Networks
6. Connecting with a Common Story
7. Connections for Opportunities and Job Advancement
8. Connections to Enhance Learning and Knowledge Sharing
9. Amplifying Influence Through Meaningful Connections
10. Connections to Console and Navigate Challenges or Distress Times
11. Connections to Fulfil Life
12. Introverts and Extroverts
13. Why do Introverts Avoid Small Talk?
14. Why Do Some People Avoid Socializing?
15. How Trust Issues Impact Communication
16. The Connectedness Corrective
17. Inability to Identify the Value of Communication
18. Chances for Establishing Connections
19. Building Meaningful Connections for Your IKIGAI
20. Connections for Adapting to Change
21. Balancing Patience and Proactivity
22. What is the reason behind our innate drive for connection?
23. Knowing Personality Types for Connection
24. What Is Effective Communication?
25. Mastering Effective Communication
26. Communication Tips for Maximum Impact

Join us on this transformative adventure and witness your life evolve into a tapestry woven with flourishing connections, boundless opportunities, and unwavering support.

Book 6 Achieve Balanced Personality
Are you ready to regain control, find your center, and navigate life's chaos with a newfound balance and resilience?
Ask yourself these five questions:
1. Why achieving balance seems elusive? Unlock the secrets to balance.
2. What lurks in the shadows of your personality, shaping your actions without your awareness? Explore your hidden self.
3. Feeling stuck in one aspect of your personality? Break free and foster holistic growth.
4. Eager to discover a clear path toward integrated growth? Find your roadmap.
5. Want practical techniques to confront and work with your shadows? Discover transformative practices for lasting change.

Unleash the power within and embark on a transformative journey with "Achieve: Balanced Personality." In this groundbreaking book, delve into the mysteries of balance, navigate the hidden realms of your personality, and break free from the constraints of one-sidedness. **Discover an integrated growth path that leads to a more complete version of yourself.**
Explore the depths of your unconscious mind as you confront the shadows within, guided by the practical techniques outlined. This book is not just about understanding; it's about taking actionable steps towards a harmonious and fulfilled life.
This book takes you through the subtopics below, unraveling intriguing insights and captivating stories.

Empower you with strategies to maintain equilibrium, ensuring resilience in facing challenges. _**Get ready to unlock the secrets to a balanced personality, confront your hidden self, and embrace a path of integrated growth.**_ This book is your guide to becoming the best version of yourself – a complete, harmonious, and resilient individual ready to navigate life with grace. **Are you prepared for the transformative journey that awaits you?**

Clear Career Inclusive Series

Book 1: Raising Your Rare Personality

Find who you are to be your best!

What is your personality type? Are you the right fit for your career? Who is a rare personality type? This book provides all the answers. Psychology is the scientific study of mind and behavior. Understand how psychology defines your unique type, growth potential, and suitable careers. Myers-Briggs Type Indicator (MBTI), a tool to identify personality typology, classifies people into 16Personalities. You can belong to any one of these 16 personality types based on your psychological preferences. Some personality types are stated as rare personality types as per MBTI. The personality type INFJ has been explored in-depth in this book. The purpose of this book is to show solidarity to who you are, identify suitable careers for all MBTI types, with a focus on the rare personality types.

Key Learnings from the book - Raising Your Rare Personality

Chapter 1 MBTI Personality Types
1. What are MBTI Personality Types?
2. How can you understand your Personality Type?
3. What are the 16Personalities?
4. Who are Rare Personality Types?
5. Who is the Rarest Personality Type?

Chapter 2 MBTI Cognitive Functions
1. What are Cognitive Functions?
2. What are the 8 Cognitive Functions?
3. What is a Primary Cognitive Function?
4. What is a Shadow Cognitive Function?
5. Cognitive Functions of all MBTI Personality Types

Chapter 3 INFJ Primary Cognitive Experiences
1. What are the Primary Cognitive Functions of an INFJ?
2. How does Introverted Intuition behave?
3. How does Extraverted Feeling behave?
4. How does Introverted Thinking behave?
5. How does Extraverted Sensing behave?

Chapter 4 INFJ Shadow Cognitive Experiences
1. What are the Shadow Cognitive functions of an INFJ?
2. How does Extroverted Intuition behave?
3. How does Introverted Feeling behave?
4. How does Extroverted Thinking behave?
5. How does Introverted Sensing behave?

Chapter 5 Rare Personality Types and Growth
1. Growth potential Function of MBTI Personality Types.
2. What are Functional Pairs?

Free Test links for finding MBTI Personality, Enneagram, Socionics, Big 5, DISC, Holland Code Job Aptitude Test, etc. are included in the book.
"A man's true delight is to do the things he was made for." – Marcus Aurelius
✓ **Find Yours!**

Book 2: Upgrade as Futuristic Empaths

Find your strength to give your best!
Are you an empath? Do you know what an empathy trap is? How can you transform empathy into a strength and build successful careers?
Empaths have intuitive feelings (owing to the cognitive functional pair "NF" in their personality type) as their psychological preference. Personality types ENFP, ENFJ, INFJ, and INFPs are natural empaths as per the **MBTI Personality types** according to www.16personalities.com and www.Truity.com. Empaths are also called **Idealists & Diplomats. Highly Sensitive People** belong to these MBTI types. To face the realities of the world and to be successful in endeavours which have larger impacts, empaths need to embrace practicality and rise above their personality stereotype or one-sidedness.
Dr.Dario Nardi, Author of the book **Neuroscience of Personality**, suggests transcendence or the individuation process, a term coined by **Carl Jung,** the essence of which is to have an integrated personality growth. Empaths have a larger role to play in this world and most of them are underplaying their natural strength.
By adopting the 5 key steps discussed in this book, anyone, especially empaths can easily find their career paths to success, thereby leaving a positive impact on this world.

Key Learnings from the book - Upgrading as Futuristic Empaths.

Chapter 1 Understanding Empaths
1. Empathic People or Empaths
2. Empathy Dilemma
3. The Value of Empathy
4. Practising Empathy
5. The Empathy Trap
6. Use of Empathy in day-to-day life
7. Empathy and Business
8. Empathy and Leadership

Chapter 2 Finding your Strength
1. Empath's Strength, Weakness & Dilemma
2. Empaths as Employees
3. Clifton Strengths
4. Machiavelli's Dilemma
5. Empath's Choice
6. Empathy as a strength in daily life
7. Fearless Empathy
8. Nurturing Empathy

Chapter 3 Developing Your Profile
1. An Empath's Growth Cognitive Function
2. Moving from One-sidedness to individuation
3. Challenges of One-sidedness for Empaths
4. The Magic Diamond for Integrated/Transcendent Judgement & Perception
5. Preferred Growth of Empaths Cognitive Functions
6. The Spiral Development of Cognitive Functions
7. Using Empathy as a Strength
8. Essentials for Building an Empath's Profile
9. Careers and Majors for Empaths

Chapter 4 Finding Your Market Niche
1. Sustainable Development Goals in Business
2. Future Job Skills
3. Selecting a Career for Empaths
4. Challenges of Workplace Toxicity
5. Future of Jobs for Empaths
6. Empaths and the Gig Economy

Chapter 5 Connecting & Networking
1. The Power of Social Connection
2. Why are we not Connecting?
3. Impact of Networking
4. Managing Digital Distraction

Chapter 6 Creating Opportunities

1. Opportunities for Empathy in Business
2. Opportunities in Sustainability
3. Empathy Revolution

"Objective judgment, now, at this very moment. Unselfish action, now, at this very moment. Willing acceptance — now, at this very moment — of all external events. That's all you need." - Marcus Aurelius

✓ **Find How!**

Book 3: Onboard as Inclusive Leaders

Find Your Potential to Impact the Best!
How Inclusive are you? Are you unconsciously biased?
Do you promote Psychological Safety?
This book will help you find answers and enable you *Onboard as Inclusive Leaders.*
Innovation, financial performance and employee productivity are indispensable for business growth. Inclusion helps in achieving these objectives of business. Diversity in line with inclusion and equity creates a sense of belonging in employees.
This book helps to develop the essential qualities required to be hired as an inclusive leader; **understand unconscious biases, the importance of psychological safety and how it has an impact on workplace productivity.**
The book also gives you the free test links to understand your MBTI personality type, strength, and Bias Tests (The Implicit Association test - Harvard University)

Key Learnings from the book:
Chapter 1 Knowing Inclusion
1. Why do we need Inclusive Leaders?
2. What is an Inclusive Workplace?
3. Features of an Inclusive Workplace
4. Challenges of Inclusive Workplace
5. Merit based Inclusion
6. Who is an inclusive leader?

Chapter 2 Inclusion Gap
1. Facts of Diversity & Inclusion
2. Microaggression
3. Unconscious Bias
4. 16 Unconscious Biases
5. Bias Test (The Implicit Association Test)

"If someone can prove me wrong and show me my mistake in any thought or action, I shall gladly change. I seek the truth, which never harmed anyone: the harm is to persist in one's own self-deception and ignorance."
— Marcus Aurelius

<u>**We need more inclusive leaders who will consider others in their decisions and that alone can give rise to sustainable development and positive impacts for people and the planet.**</u>

√**Find How**

Acknowledgement

My gratitude to the readers of my book, for your time and reviews, and to all my well-wishers for your support. I am indebted to all who reached out to me with feedback and input. I have to start by thanking my family, friends, and classmates for their encouragement, counsel, and good-natured jibes. Extending my wholehearted gratitude to everyone on the Author Freedom Hub, special thanks to Som Bathla for his vote of confidence and my fellow authors for their unbounded support. To Anita Jocelyn for her editorial help towards the completion of my book. I am grateful to Mr. Sareej for his efforts towards the beautiful cover design. I thank my friends and colleagues who helped me with their insights and experiences of their work place inclusion. Your inputs were critical in the completion of this book and helped me gather information to cover this topic in details for my readers. In no way at all the least, I am very thankful to my spouse Jo and our son Yakob for helping me out immensely by allowing me space and time to pursue my interests and creating a conducive environment to achieve my goals. To my mother Prof. Thresiamma Sunny, I am thankful for her unwavering support and inspiration to always deliver my best.

I could not have done it without you all.

References

Chapter 1

1. India's 'Lake Man' Relies on Ancient Methods to Ease a Water Crisis - The New York Times (nytimes.com)
2. Anand Malligavad: Restoring the lakes glory | TED Talk
3. The Four Faces of Empathy: Understanding and Cultivating Different Types of Empathy | by Mindful Engineer | Medium
4. Empathy - Wikipedia
5. The Differences Between Empaths and Highly Sensitive People (drjudithorloff.com)
6. 10 Traits Empathic People Share | Psychology Today
7. Empathic Intelligence I Ideos Institute
8. There Are 9 Types of Intelligence - Which One Fits Your Personality Type? | True You Journal (truity.com)
9. What Is Empathy and Why Is It So Important in Design Thinking? | IxDF (interaction-design.org)

Chapter 2

1. Why Maya Angelou Stopped Speaking and How She Found Her Voice Again (goalcast.com)
2. Sensory processing sensitivity - Wikipedia
3. Mirror Neurons and the Neuroscience of Empathy (positivepsychology.com)
4. 14 Problems Only Empaths Will Understand | Highly Sensitive Refuge
5. 'I feel your pain': confessions of a hyper-empath | Health & wellbeing | The Guardian
6. 'I Feel Your Pain': The Neuroscience of Empathy – Association for Psychological Science – APS

7. 7 Ways Empaths Can Heal From Trauma and PTSD | Psychology Today

Chapter 3

1. https://indianexpress.com/article/sports/cricket-world-cup/depression-low-to-double-ton-high-glenn-maxwell-powers-australia-victory-9018074/
2. Glenn Maxwell details his mental health demons (smh.com.au)
3. Being Highly Sensitive Is A Superpower - Here's How To Leverage It (forbes.com)
4. Why Being Sensitive Is a Strength | TIME
5. These 8 Skills Will Help You Thrive as a Highly Sensitive Person (highlysensitiverefuge.com)
6. How vulnerability, empathy, and authenticity reshape modern leadership (forbes.com)
7. Intuition Is The Highest Form Of Intelligence (forbes.com)
8. How Sensitivity Is Linked to Brilliance | Psychology Today
9. Sensitivity: The Most Elegant Kind of Intelligence - Exploring your mind
10. 7 common traits of highly intelligent people | World Economic Forum (weforum.org)
11. How to Stay Empathic Without Suffering So Much (berkeley.edu)
12. How to Develop and Strengthen Your Empathy | Psychology Today

Chapter 4

1. The Day Mahatma Gandhi Threw His Sandal Off A Train | Tom Rapsas (patheos.com)
2. 12 Reasons Being a Highly Sensitive Person Is Your Greatest Strength at Work | Psychology Today
3. Practical Empathy | 2024 Global Culture Report | O.C. Tanner (octanner.com)

Made in the USA
Monee, IL
06 December 2024